The Charismatic Bond

The Charismatic Bond

Political Behavior in Time of Crisis

Douglas Madsen and Peter G. Snow

Harvard University Press
Cambridge, Massachusetts
London, England
1991

This book is printed on acid-free paper, and its binding materials
have been chosen for strength and durability.

Library of Congress Cataloging-in-Publication Data
Madsen, Douglas.
The charismatic bond : political behavior in time of crisis /
Douglas Madsen and Peter G. Snow.
p.   cm.
Includes bibliographical references and index.
ISBN 0–674–10987–2 (acid-free paper)
1. Perón, Juan Domingo, 1895–1974—Psychology. 2. Charisma
(Personality trait) 3. Peronism—History. I. Snow, Peter G.
II. Title.
F2849.P48M28 1991
982.06′2′092—dc20
90–27256
CIP

For Joanie and Ingrid, Andy and Judy

Acknowledgments

We are grateful to many people for their contributions to our research: to Jeane Kirkpatrick, Lars Schoultz, and Peter Smith for providing their data sets for our further analysis; to the Librarian of the Dirección Nacional de Estadística y Censos for digging out unpublished 1946 census data; to the Section Chief of the Departamento Electoral, Ministerio del Interior, for providing us with key precinct voting data for the 1980s; to Katherine Newcomer for able research assistance; to Gerhard Loewenberg, Donald McCrone, Arthur Miller, and James Stimson for critiquing various portions of the manuscript. Financial assistance was provided by the Henry and Grace Doherty Foundation, the American Philosophical Society, the Fulbright Commission, and the University of Iowa. All translations from the Spanish, unless otherwise indicated, are by the authors.

Contents

Figures

Tables

★ 1 ★

On the Appearance and
Evolution of Charisma

The empirical study of charisma has been shaped by a general definition of the term which, though well grounded etymologically, has had the effect of leading research into an intellectual blind alley. Reflecting the term's Greek root (usually translated as "gift of grace"), this definition identifies charisma as a very rare virtue, power, or talent which endows its holder with various capacities, most notably one for eliciting passionate popular support for a mission or for the holder's guidance in human affairs. Often the definition also ties charisma to a divine, or in some other sense ultimate, source. But whether the emphasis be sacred or secular, the key point is that charisma has been seen as something *possessed* by certain extraordinary individuals—Lenin, Hitler, Gandhi, Perón.

Typical in this regard is the perspective offered by Dean Keith Simonton, who writes: "Few personality traits are more resistant to precise definition than is charisma. To be charismatic is to possess some mysterious attribute that provides the foundation of exceptional influence, whether that influence is exerted in intimate interpersonal contacts or before immense crowds of people."[1] Notice where attention is directed: to the leader's personality traits or to personal attributes. Missing from this perspective, and from most work on charisma, is equal concern with the specific context in which charisma arises and, relatedly, with the exact nature of the following which rallies to the emergent leader's banner.

Guided by such definitional emphases—and perhaps unwittingly influenced by the inappropriate use of the term by commentators describing popular figures in contemporary life—empirical investigators of charisma have focused their efforts on discovering what it is about particular individuals which endows them with this mysterious quality. What are their special personality features? What unusual skills do they have? Might some physical characteristic be important? Can peculiar formative experiences be identified? Attempts to answer such questions have led to intensive study of the lives of one or more purportedly charismatic individuals—the hope of the single-case student being that generalizations will be suggested and the hope of the comparativist being that commonalities will be found.

Neglect of context and following has not been total, of course. For more than fifty years, virtually all academic work on charisma has been grounded in the theorizing of Max Weber, who plainly understood the importance of both and in an often-cited passage gave special attention to the latter: "The term charisma will be applied to a certain quality of an individual personality by virtue of which he is set apart from ordinary men and treated as endowed with supernatural, superhuman, or at least specifically exceptional powers or qualities. . . . It is the recognition on the part of those subject to authority which is decisive for the validity of charisma. This is freely given . . . and consists in devotions . . . hero worship, or absolute trust in the leader."[2]

Great emphasis must be put on the point that it is the emergent following which sets the charismatic figure apart from ordinary mortals and which treats that figure as specially endowed. And this happens in a special context. In most general terms it is a context which has special impact upon those who come to respond to the charismatic leader, but in Weber's theory of history it was further specified as a context of social and economic crisis and institutional breakdown.[3]

Given Weber's sweeping theoretical concerns, it is not surprising that he was quite general in his discussion of the particulars of context and following. Yet it may be that this generality set the stage for the current condition of charisma research, in which such matters are given only passing acknowledgment and virtually no empirical specification. Even investigators who take theoretical note of questions about following and context too often at the operational stage of their research lapse back into the kind of personality or attribute studies which simply cannot succeed in illuminating charismatic phenomena.[4]

Among other reasons for the failure of attribute studies is the research design itself. If one studies only (supposedly) charismatic leaders, there is no variance in the dependent variable. Charisma is a constant. Hence personality variables, for example, cannot be tied to the charismatic outcomes. Variables do not explain constants. Moreover, even if common and invariant attributes of charismatic leaders could be identified, there would remain no causal connection with charisma unless it could be shown that *only* charismatic figures have those features, something that cannot be shown using this design. In other words, one might stumble onto a necessary condition but could never show it to be a sufficient one. This situation can lead to paradoxical findings to the effect that all charismatic leaders have a particular feature—an aggressive personality, say— but that almost no one with that feature ever becomes a charismatic leader.

What is more, this type of search for special attributes of charismatic figures is wholly in the dark. Neglecting the followers who resonate to one or another of those attributes (in a particular context), investigators can only guess about which of them have placed that figure at center stage and which of them, perhaps not the same, can keep him there.

Such endeavors are reminiscent of the futile search by social psychologists for general leadership traits, a search finally abandoned after the scrutiny of countless cases and the accumulation of volumes of speculative theorizing failed to yield any substantial result.[5] In the end, however, the null finding was important. First, it led to the conclusion that when it comes to leadership, there is no man or woman for all seasons; hence, the search for context-free leadership traits should be abandoned.[6] Second, it underscored the need to investigate leadership as a relational phenomenon— that is, as a phenomenon in which the special qualities of a particular leader are meshed with the special features of his or her following.

In spite of their relevance, these lessons seem largely to have been passed over by students of political charisma, possibly because of a gulf between the two social science sectors within which the different research traditions developed. More difficult to understand is the neglect of important conceptual work on the nature of influence in the literature of political science itself. More than forty years ago, Harold Lasswell wrote in *Power and Personality:*

> The accent is on power and the powerful. But it would be a mistake to imagine that in consequence we are wholly taken up with the few rather than the many. Speaking of power and the powerful is an ellipsis, leaving out what is perhaps the longest arc of the circle constituting a power relation. . . . Power is an interpersonal situation; those who hold power are empowered. They depend upon and continue only so long as there is a continuing stream of empowering responses. Even a casual inspection of human relations will convince any competent observer that power is not a brick that can be lugged from place to place, but a process that vanishes when the supporting responses cease.[7]

Lasswell's argument requires the empiricist working on political influence to give systematic attention not just to the leader but perhaps even more to the followers (though, it must be admitted, Lasswell himself did not undertake such research). What is it *in the followers* which responds to the leader's performance? This perspective was elaborated in broader and more systematic fashion in the important conceptual analysis of political influence developed by Robert Dahl.[8] Dahl's point of departure is that all influence terms refer to relationships. Of course, nothing is more obvious than that there can be no leaders without followers, no dominants without subordinates. Thus, at the level of common sense there has long been recognition of the relational nature of influence. But it apparently has been much less obvious that every such relationship says something important about both of its complementary elements, something about the influencer and something at least as important about the responder(s). If a leader is magnetic, then something about the following is magnetizable. Any statement describing an actor simply as influential is all but meaningless. Influential over whom? With respect to what? And in what context? The student of influence must carefully specify, for any particular demonstration of influence, the nature of the audience. What is its makeup, demographic and psychological? What does that audience see in this influential actor? In truth, close study of this audience of followers may be even more important than close study of the leader's performance, since in a strict sense it is the followers' perception of that performance, rather than the performance itself, which bonds them to the leader.

Charisma Defined

Charisma is an influence term. This point must be clearly understood. Thus, all of the lessons which apply to the study of influence in general also apply to the study of charisma in particular. And any definition of charisma which neglects the relational aspect of the phenomenon, which focuses attention almost entirely on leaders, misdirects empirical research.

How, then, is charisma to be defined? In plainest language, it is an influence relationship marked by asymmetry, directness, and, for the follower, great passion. Asymmetry means that the leader has profound influence on attitudes and behavior of the following but that the opposite is not true; the following does provide the all-important empowering responses, to use Lasswell's terminology, but its other influence on the leader is muted. Directness means the absence of significant mediation of the relationship, by either formal structures or informal networks. Great passion is a little more difficult to define. It is much more than the feeling an audience associates with "popular" public figures—although the term charisma is often (and almost always, wrongly) applied to such figures. Indeed, it is much more than many of us have ever experienced in dealing with leaders of one kind or another. Great passion means intense devotion to and extraordinary reverence for the leader. Of the three defining elements, it obviously is this which is most distinctive of charisma. And it also is this which is most fascinating as a focus for behavioral analysis.

Some theorists would dispute any contention that charisma is an influence relationship different only in degree of passion from many other such relationships. Ann Ruth Wilner,[9] for example, argues that charisma is different *in kind* because followers in a charismatic bond (1) attribute to the leader truly extraordinary and heroic qualities; (2) exhibit blind and unreasoning faith and obedience; and (3) attach themselves to the leader with total emotional commitment. Were charismatic influence sui generis it would mean that empirical work on charisma would stand alone, cut off from the research literature treating other forms of influence. In fact, however, there is no systematic research whatsoever underpinning the difference-in-kind argument; and even at the conceptual level the argument seems odd. Extreme positions on three variables do not provide a logical basis for such an argument. Moreover, underlying all three factors, in our judgment, is the intensity of the emotional bond with the leader. It is this which feeds the attributions of godliness and the seemingly blind faith and obedience. And while it is true that such emotionality, by definition, is peculiar to charisma, it is not the case that there is no counterpart (though obviously a paler and less dramatic one) in other types of influence relationships. Emotionality, after all, is a continuum, not a dichotomy.

For some commentators an essential element in the definition of charisma is "irrationality."[10] Perhaps because of an initial grounding of the concept in mystical experience—and perhaps also because of Weber's use of such dramatic examples as berserkers and "epileptoid" shamans—charisma is seen as necessarily involving an irrational response by the mass to the leader. This is a point of importance and worth special attention here.

At the outset, one must note that the meaning of rationality (or its opposite) is not straightforward in these discussions—nor, for that matter, in general. Sidney Winter[11] identifies six logically independent connotations of rationality in positive behavior theory: consistent choice, conformity between goals/beliefs and behavior, creative problem solving, sound decision procedures, pursuit of viability or survival, and advanced learning ability. That these connotations may conflict with one another is plain. Winter notes, for example, "in a changing environment, creativity may be required for viability, but may be incompatible with consistency, and perhaps with conformity and sound procedure."[12] Ultimately, he falls back on a situational definition of rationality, one having different emphases in different contexts but which has at its core the pursuit of self-interest.

Irrationality as a topic in discussions of charisma is much less systematically considered. Two interrelated elements are commonly implied: an impulsiveness and an absence of sound reasoning. The former deals with choices or actions which are deemed too quick, too undeliberative to be effective in serving self-interest. The latter deals with choices or actions which are deemed wrong-headed in terms of method or effect and therefore out of keeping with self-interest. In both cases what is meant is self-interest *properly conceived*, a point to which we will return.

Irrationality very often is blamed on emotions. For example, it might be argued that impulsiveness is driven by fear; or that sound reasoning is blocked by anxieties which arise when such reasoning threatens to break down core beliefs or values. But note that such arguments, conventional in both the behavioral sciences and in everyday life, assign to ratiocination the principal, even the entire, responsibility for effective pursuit of self-interest. Fear or anxieties —indeed, emotions in general—are seen as somehow counter-productive.

A moment's thought reveals the absurdity of a belief that emotions only get in the way when pursuing self-interest—if what we mean by self-interest is survival. It is not only by sound reasoning that the human organism copes with challenge; some important mechanisms of physical response do not engage the cerebral cortex at all. And most assuredly, it is not only by sound reasoning that our social existence is maintained. Bondings between humans, as with parents and children, soldiers in combat units, or entire national communities, are not left to cost-benefit analysis, even though such cognitive appraisals indisputably play a role. And with respect to the very root of behavior, motivation, it is clear that our inducements are neither established nor, often, much governed by cerebral processes. R. B. Zajonc,[13] upon reviewing much evidence, concludes that emotions are primary, basic, and inescapable (a wholly unsurprising argument if applied to any other animal, but no other animal is ever described as "irrational").

In this larger rationality, then, a crucial role is assigned to emotions and other brain functions which are only peripherally related to conscious reasoning. Put differently, though we are generally loath to admit it (since it disturbingly constrains our sense of efficacy), humans are playing a survival game which is only partially, perhaps even secondarily, connected to ratiocination. Emotions have never been shown in general to get in the way of play in this game; indeed, they are at the heart of it. This is not to say that emotions always and everywhere enhance effective choice and action; only that normally they contribute to adaptive—and therefore, rational—behavior.

Finally, as noted above, irrationality is attributed to actors who behave in a fashion out of keeping with self-interest. However, departures from the pursuit of self-interest can never be shown to have occurred. An individual retrospectively judging his or her own behavior as irrational, usually after a personal reversal of one sort or another, has moved into a new context with new standards. Outsiders making the same judgment are merely invoking their own rules and understandings. In both cases, the charge of irrationality is grounded in the belief that the actors did not correctly see what their true self-interests were, for reasons of emotionality, false consciousness, faulty heuristics, or whatever, and therefore their actions are deemed inappropriate. (Note that errors in calculation or flaws in method are not in themselves sufficient to establish a failure in pursuit of self-interest.) That there is a proper conception of self-interest is here no more than a convenient and empirically unwarranted assumption. On the one hand, it allows the positive theorist to proceed, usually at the aggregate level, without delving into the particulars of actual motivation. On the other, it permits the ideologically committed to assert superior knowledge of (and often to claim a privileged role in) human affairs.

Coming back to charisma, one can see that although intense

emotion is a hallmark of charismatic influence, it does not therefore follow that the mass response is in some way "irrational." This is true with respect to the reasoning of the followers, which would have to be assessed (somehow) empirically, and it is more obviously true with respect to their pursuit of self-interest more broadly conceived. Indeed, even an amalgam of weak or flawed ratiocination and strong emotions, were it to be found in charismatic followers, would not constitute evidence of a failure to pursue self-interest.

In the final analysis, the use of irrationality (or rationality) as concepts in the study of charisma can only breed confusion and obscure actualities. As is usually the case, the jettisoning of such global labels and the identification and measurement of particular variables—here, perceptual and emotional variables—will much improve the research enterprise.

A Psychological Theory of Charismatic Bonding

Weber's views on the origins of charisma have been little advanced in the research they have spawned. As noted earlier, his general argument—that social crisis and institutional breakdown set the stage for the rise of a charismatic leader—is widely accepted. But how crisis and breakdown work their effects, upon whom, and under what conditions are left largely unspecified, both theoretically and empirically, by students of charisma. Instead, the common practice has been to assume the domain and scope (to use Dahl's terms) of the charismatic influence in point so as to get on with what is mistakenly believed to be the more important investigative concern: exploring the particulars of the leader's life.[14]

Purely serendipitously, a major step in filling this theoretical vacuum has been taken by Albert Bandura,[15] who, though having no apparent concern with charismatic phenomena, nonetheless has developed a general and powerful theory of human coping behavior which speaks directly to the problem at hand. His theory, supported by an impressive body of evidence from both laboratory and field studies (including a substantial amount emerging from Bandura's own research program), assigns a fundamental place to *self-efficacy*

—the subjective assessment of one's own capacity to deal with environmentally-posed challenges.

The essence of the theory is that self-referent thought in general and self-efficacy judgments in particular mediate the relationship between knowledge and action, affecting both motivation and behavior. Feelings of self-efficacy strongly influence all coping efforts as well as diverse other phenomena, including physiological stress reactions, thought patterns, and emotional responses. People who perceive themselves to be efficacious are prepared resolutely to confront environmental demands. But perceived self-efficacy (combined with suitable motivation) does not by itself determine whether coping behavior will be undertaken; also crucial are judgments of the relevant environment. For example, one may believe oneself to be personally effective but feel that the environment inhibits or blocks the possibilities for successful action. Success or failure is thus seen as dependent upon some combination of self-efficacy and environmental circumstance. Very often it can only be a matter of assumption what contribution to an outcome is made by each part of that combination.

Perceived self-efficacy, the theory continues, is the product of social learning. In that learning, four sources of information are important: (1) the outcomes from one's own performances, (2) vicarious experience of others' performances, (3) verbal persuasion, and (4) one's own physiological states. It should be underscored that the first is the most influential of the four. However, in some important domains, especially those removed from everyday life, the first is almost irrelevant; direct tests of self-efficacy are missing and individuals assume their capabilities on the basis of vicarious or otherwise persuasive efficacy information. This can be important for the stability of this self-assessment. As a rule, direct tests provide the strongest evidence of capacity and therefore buttress confidence in a perception of self-efficacy. Where such tests have not occurred, that perception is likely to be somewhat more fragile.

This is not to say that one's "tests" are unbiased.[16] The sense of personal efficacy, whether global or topical, is often so intimately linked to self-esteem that positive conclusions about that efficacy are less a matter of judgment than they are of desire. Unmistakable successes plainly facilitate such positive conclusions, but so can ambiguous results, if "translated" into successes by needy egos. In any event, the accumulation of successes, real or imagined, enhances the stability of self-efficacy and blunts the capacity of new evidence to undermine it. But obviously not everyone will experience successes, either directly or vicariously, in spite of the effort to find such outcomes, thereby supporting derivative conclusions about positive self-efficacy. Self-efficacy will vary from person to person —and also from culture to culture and from era to era.

There is good evidence that perceptions of self-efficacy and perceptions of environmental responsiveness develop differently, though not entirely separately, and that it is the positive version of the former which is the most easily taught and maintained.[17] Moreover, with respect to the uncertainty commonly to be found in determining the part played by self and that played by environment in producing particular outcomes, the general tendency appears to be self-congratulatory if the outcome is positive but self-exonerating if the outcome is negative (in which case the environment is likely to be blamed). Such a bias in favor of positive self-efficacy is in keeping with the view that such perceptions are valued and actively defended.

Sometimes the psychic defense of positive self-efficacy becomes difficult. When negative "test" results override defenses, they can ultimately erode the sense of coping ability even in strong believers. One obvious way to defend self-image under these conditions is to assume that it is the environment which has changed; one's own capacity remains but conditions have turned sour. This explanation may itself be undermined, however, by evidence of success for relevant others. Thus, it might be a relief, at least initially, to find that one is *not* unique in experiencing failure, that many relevant others are in the same boat. This leaves the self-image intact. However, such psychic relief has limited value in domains having to do with fundamental needs. When survival is involved, it helps little to discover that all are failing.

Bandura finds that judgments of self-efficacy and judgments of environmental responsiveness have quite different behavioral and emotional implications. When both are positive—that is, when the self is seen as capable and the environment as responsive—the result (motivation assumed) is assured, timely action. When both are negative, the result is apathy. But when the self is perceived positively and the environment negatively, protest or milieu change is to be expected—one seeks to change or escape from the offending environment. And finally, when a negative view of self is joined to a positive view of the environment, the result is self-devaluation and despondency.

These behavioral and emotional responses are for steady-state conditions and sure attributions. For our purposes, however, it is as interesting to consider transitional states and their accompanying uncertainties. What happens when circumstances change and, in particular, when a positive sense of efficacy vis-à-vis one's fundamental needs is threatened by events? Because fundamental needs are involved, one probably cannot simply shrug off or rationalize failures. The initial response, as noted above, probably will be that least damaging to sense of self—namely, to blame the environment and to seek to change or escape its effects. The presumption here is that effective action of some sort is still possible. But if that effort ultimately fails and, in the midst of uncertainty and confusion, one begins to entertain thoughts of *personal* inefficacy, the response for many probably will change; action will give way to inaction, and anger will give way to despair.[18]

The relevance of this psychological theory for the analysis of charismatic bonding becomes clear when we consider the human meaning of social and institutional breakdown. The collapse of a great social enterprise, such as a polity or an economy, brings with it for many (but not all) of those involved a collapse of their own personal worlds. Expectations are dashed and hopes ruined. Fundamental assumptions are undermined. Social arrangements and economic structures disintegrate. Often "understanding" is lost and, with it, the sense of being able to cope. In many of the areas where self-efficacy seemed strongest and most justified, one's efforts to deal with crucial problems repeatedly fail.

Since one's own performance attainments most strongly influence perceptions of self-efficacy, we can surmise that a context in which the most elemental, familiar, and important performances fail will be a context in which self-efficacy feelings also are likely to fail. A concrete example of such failure is a situation in which long-established ways of gaining food and shelter no longer work and survival itself may seem to be in doubt. After initially blaming environmental circumstance, many victims who experience continued failure in coping efforts—quite likely in the sort of general crisis Weber spoke of—will experience doubts about self. Anger then is mixed with fear. Moreover, vicarious experience reinforces negative perceptions. In a general collapse, visible failure can be found everywhere.

It is important to reflect on the stressful consequences of ubiquitous failure in these circumstances, for it has the effect of accelerating the collapse of self-efficacy more generally. If such psychological reversals are not common, one might expect social networks to blunt their effects; the "disabled" individuals might fall back on family and friends and find persuasive reason to avoid personal recrimination. However, where such reversals are wholesale and where they occur in areas of fundamental need, these networks can offer no solace; the collapse of perceived efficacy is collective rather than individual. The set of relevant others is sinking together. And, for that reason, the effects for each individual involved are accelerated and made worse. The end point is despair.

This is not to say that the process is invariant across the affected population. There always is variance in a population's convictions about self-efficacy, whether positive or negative. For some individuals, a change in self-image requires a great deal of persuasive evidence; for others, it takes relatively little. Hence, when catastrophic change hits a society, some people fall into despair quickly, but others do not. The latter group, however, is not unaffected, and its resilience should not be taken as immunity.

We find it useful to think of self-efficacy as normally distributed, both in good times and in bad, for any large population. In good times, most people are coping relatively effectively and only the lower tail of the distribution is in crisis. In bad times, the entire distribution shifts downward, bringing many more people into the crisis zone.

The Retreat to "Proxy Control"

The psychological stress associated with a perceived loss of control is well documented.[19] With respect to large-scale social or economic breakdown, such stress at first may be muted by a persistent sense of personal efficacy (since the environment is being blamed for failures) and by the purposive actions this perception sustains. This muting will be relatively short-lived, however, given the ever more apparent loss of control, personally and collectively, in the midst of crisis. Stress levels then are sure to rise. It might be that a sort of escape can be found in apathy—the theoretical expectation for a fully negative view of self-efficacy in a hostile environment—but apathy with respect to the fundamental needs of life seems a terminal condition. Especially for those whose world has collapsed, in contrast with those who have never known such a world, apathy must be much less likely than anger and then finally despair.

The sense of lost control and the despair which accompanies it create the possibility of a retreat to what Bandura calls "proxy control." He describes this condition in the following terms:

> People are not averse to relinquishing control over events that affect their lives in order to free themselves of the performance demands and hazards that the exercise of control entails. Rather than seeking personal control, they seek their security in proxy control—wherein they can exert some influence over those who wield influence and power. Part of the price of proxy control is restriction of one's own efficacy and a vulnerable security that rests on the competencies and favors of others. . . . [T]hose who believe themselves to be less skilled readily yield control to others to cope with the aversive environment. The dependent ones enjoy the protective benefits without the performance demands and attendant stresses.[20]

The acceptance of proxy control as a psychologically self-preserving strategy goes to the very heart of the charismatic bond. In this process those in despair restore their own sense of coping ability by linking themselves to a dominant and seemingly effective figure—a leader who seems to be acting in their behalf, but also seems to be not beyond their influence (if only because that leader is "known" to be devoted to their interests and therefore reachable through petition and supplication).[21] This process also can be described in the somewhat more familiar terms of psychoanalytic theory: the collapse of efficacy and the erosion of self-esteem bring a regression of personality which leads the despairing to seek a restoration of their attachment to a "father" as the ego ideal. When such a figure is found, this bonding grows stronger as followers subordinate their sense of self to the ego of the leader and in the process develop a group identification. The bonding with the leader, and also with the group, restores a sense of security and of competency, which ultimately may provide the foundation for renewed autonomy.[22]

Whatever the deeper psychological processes involved here, it is clear that there is something of a paradox in the entire process: only by yielding personal control is a sense of control retained; only by accepting the leader's "understanding" of events is a sense of personal understanding restored. In any event, because it is profoundly relieving, such bonding is accompanied by very strong positive emotion—the crucial feature of charisma. It is important to note that this relief from stress and fear is itself a reinforcer of commitment. Although the initial belief in the leader surely must be inspired by at least some hint of a real ability to deal with the followers' problems, once faith is in place the relief it brings with it makes that faith itself something of great positive value, something to be held onto and conserved (in the same sense that an ideology may be held onto and conserved). Hence, the actual performances of the leader thereafter become even less accurately perceivable by a following which almost desperately wishes to believe. Of course, it must be added that there are limits to what even fervent commitment can gloss over or obscure.

We do not wish to argue that proxy control will only be found in settings of high stress. Robert Lane, for example, finds that some apparently ordinary people exhibit a "fear of equality" and believe that it can be "comforting to have the 'natural leaders' of a society well entrenched in their proper place. If there were equality there would no longer be such an elite to supervise and take care of people—especially 'me.'"[23] But in the midst of general crisis and breakdown this sentiment is likely to become much more common. Large numbers of people may then come to seek psychic and material salvation in a retreat to proxy control.

Note that the connection of severe psychological stress with this bonding process does not require that the leader-follower relationship be broadly political or public in character. Some personal crises may aggregate to macroscopic proportions, as in the circumstances Weber wrote about; others may remain microscopic, more likely to be addressed by clergy or psychiatrists than studied by social scientists. At the macroscopic end of the continuum, the leader who is charismatically bonded with a mass following will be highly visible and broadly political. However, leader-follower bonds found further down the continuum—for example, within chiliastic sects —or even bonds found at the microscopic end—for example, between patient and psychiatrist—may also be charismatic.

For some facing degeneration of perceived coping ability, salvation may be found less in a powerful leader than in a powerful, millenarian, and action-oriented ideology and its accompanying movement. Arthur Koestler, for example, writes of his conversion to communism: "I became converted because I was ripe for it and lived in a disintegrating society thirsting for faith. . . . Every page of Marx, and even more of Engels, brought a new revelation and an intellectual delight. . . . a mood of emotional fervor and intellectual bliss. . . . The new star of Bethlehem had risen in the East. . . . Something had clicked in my brain which shook me like a mental explosion. To say that one had seen the light is a poor description of the mental rapture which only the convert knows."[24] Communist Party members interviewed by Hadley Cantril in France and Italy also speak of their affiliation: "Only those of us who have the guidance of the Party know what we can best do in our day-to-day activities to carry on the fight against the exploitation of workers" (from a French industrial worker). "The Communist Party has always been interested in my personal well-being. In fact, if I get work at all, I owe it to the comrades of the Party" (Italian farm worker). "Marxism is a science; no doubt about it. . . . Marxism gives us power" (French local labor leader). "When the future society of Communism arrives it will be so wonderful—we have no doubts about it. We hardly dare believe it. There will be no more exploitation. There will be no more conflicts" (French Party worker).[25]

Of course, the general theme in all of this is a familiar one: I was lost, but with my conversion I am found; I was wandering, confused, and without hope, but with my conversion I am saved and know the way. Roland Warren[26] finds this theme very prominent in Christian hymns and, interestingly, also in the *Parteilieder* of National Socialist Germany. And in the spate of contemporary accounts of conversion to modern religious cults the theme is ubiquitous. Christopher Edwards describes first his sense of being lost, marked by a growing sense of nihilism and futility while a student at Yale University and ultimately by the belief that: "All my gods had finally fallen, casting me adrift in a world without love or direction. . . . God seemed my only hope, my sole chance." Then comes the search for salvation: "I was prepared to do anything to shed my past fears and misunderstandings. . . . I was determined to search, to go anywhere. . . . And I desperately hoped that, if there was a God of love, there were others like myself with whom I could share my desires." Finally, there is the conversion, this time to the Unification Church of Sun Myung Moon: "Tears streamed down my face, tears of joy or sadness, or God knows what in this chaotic caldron of unbridled emotion. I was a little child once again. . . . The Family [other church members] kept jostling me, elbowing me, shaking my hand. Nobody had ever loved me so much, nobody had really cared. . . . This was where I wanted to stay, where I could be loved and accepted. This was the place where God wanted me to be." And in the midst of an emotional group audience with the leader, Rev. Moon: "suddenly it was all so clear. God did have a plan and only Father [Moon] knew it. All we had to do was follow Father—that was it—that was all! The world was turning to Father for help and all the seeds that had been planted would soon be ready."[27]

The theme also emerges from some of the autobiographical sketches of early Nazis collected by Theodore Abel[28] and reanalyzed by Peter Merkl.[29] One young man, returning from war, writes: "The sad pictures of red rule we saw while marching back deeply depressed us frontline soldiers. We just could not and would not understand that this was the upshot of four-and-a-half years of our struggle. . . . The homeland had become so alien and un-German to me and I felt a longing and desire for a new order which . . . would resurrect the tormented fatherland in better and wonderful ways."[30] And another early follower of Hitler comments more pointedly:

> One often hears the question why it was that youth spontaneously rallied to Hitler. But the experiences of war, revolution, and inflation supply an explanation. We were not spared anything. We knew and felt the worries in the house [as children]. The shadow of necessity never left our table and made us silent. We were rudely pushed out of our childhood and not shown the right path. The struggle for life got to us early. Misery, shame, hatred, lies, and civil war imprinted themselves on our souls. . . . So we searched and found Adolf Hitler.[31]

Obviously, such autobiographical accounts can be no more than illustrative. Presentations of self by a wholly unrepresentative sample of true believers cannot by themselves be taken as the basis for firm conclusions. Yet what is striking in all of this is the ubiquitous nature of the essential theme when personal crises are at hand.

The retreat to proxy control in the midst of crisis can take more than one form. At the one extreme the proxy is wholly personalized and ideologically empty. At the other the proxy is purely ideological, but no doubt connected to proselytizing agents and probably connected to a mass following. And in the middle, exemplified by the religious case, there is an amalgam of ideology, movement, and (otherworldly) leader. For ideology to be involved, it must be suitable to the context and relatively well propagated. Where such an ideology is missing, surely very common when perceptions of self-efficacy quite suddenly become matters of doubt, the personalist form of proxy control is the only one available. It must be underscored, however, that exact knowledge about these processes is lacking and that political conversions remain a subject greatly in need of systematic empirical research.

Social Effects of Psychological Stress

What is better understood is the social response to stressful circumstances. Two rather different kinds of evidence speak to this. The first is from large-scale survey studies and the second, from smaller group investigations. The survey studies deal with U.S. data. One pertinent finding is that individuals who feel themselves unable to understand and cope with political events, compared with those who do feel able in that respect, are more likely to endorse authoritarian solutions to their society's problems.[32] This result is nicely in keeping with the proxy control argument.

The second survey-based finding is derived from time-series analysis of presidential popularity data and also speaks, though a bit indistinctly, to the matter of proxy control in stressful times. Specifically, the finding is that public opinion exhibits a significant "rally-round-the-leadership" response in times of international crisis. With other confounding factors statistically controlled, there is a highly visible crisis effect which boosts the popularity rating of incumbent presidents. Such a crisis-driven response is in keeping with the old maxim about strength accruing (at least in the short run) to the political leader who takes the nation into war. But there surely is a commingling here of feelings of nationalist solidarity and feelings of leader support. The extent of each cannot be assessed.

Smaller group studies also contribute to our understanding of the social response to stressful circumstances. One well-established finding from such studies is that groups entering into intense competition with rivals develop autocratic power structures, and do so with what appears to be full acceptance by the membership. This

has been found in field research[33] as well as in laboratory investigations.[34] The key point is that the emergence of the strong leader
is not contested; the other members fall into line and accept the
role of followers in a way that suggests, if not relief, at least the
absence of qualms.

What does intense competition do to produce such a change in
social structure? The physiological effects are at the surface level
reasonably well understood. What is involved has been described
as a stress-induced endocrine cascade, in which, through a variety
of complex mechanisms, the individual is readied for action.[35]
Although the exact relationship between this physiological stress
reaction and psychological feelings cannot be spelled out, the view
that the two operate in tandem is not a matter for doubt. Hence
one can again point to the linkage between stress and acceptance
of strong leadership.

A related finding is that psychological stress (this time, directly
measured) increases individual motivation to affiliate with—and to
express solidarity with—social units. This has been seen in small-
group laboratory studies,[36] in investigations of soldiers in combat,[37]
in research on children living under the threat of war,[38] and in
research on natural disasters.[39] It also constitutes the foundation of
what Irving Janis[40] calls "groupthink." Fear[41] and threat[42] apparently have the same effect. But the key point is that those facing
such stressful conditions not only want to affiliate with others but
prefer groups with strong leaders over those without them.[43] Affiliation appears to reduce the debilitating effects of severe stress,[44]
and affiliation with groups having strong leaders appears to be
especially effective both in reducing stress and in actually coping
with the problems at hand.[45] Once again, the evidence suggests
that stressful circumstances ready people for strong leadership.

The final bit of evidence from smaller groups, provided by Robert
Hamblin,[46] ties neatly in with the other findings. What he has
shown is that a crisis in confidence among problem-solving groups
has the effect of concentrating influence in fewer hands than had
been the case beforehand. In other words, when group members
feel they have lost their way, group structure changes in much the

same way that it changes under intense competition. As with the stress effects discussed above, this seems to be a case in which self-efficacy feelings are weakened. Passing influence to others here can be interpreted as a resort to proxy control (which, if it failed, would in this theory be only a way station en route to apathy).

Taken together, these studies constitute a reasonably strong body of evidence connecting stressful circumstances with a preference for strong leaders. The evidence comes from large survey studies, of both cross-sectional and time-series design, and from smaller group studies. The linkage between stressful circumstances and the desire for strong leadership is no surprise from the perspective of Weberian theory. What is new here is Bandura's specification of a psychological theory which accounts for the development of that linkage. Self-efficacy theory provides a powerful organizing scheme for the study of charisma in its initial stages. A wide range of findings can be subsumed under its interpretative rules. The psychological process which leads individuals to become seekers, ready to fall back on proxy control and to be enthralled by a leader, is persuasively laid out.

What self-efficacy theory cannot do, however, is explain why a particular "proxy" is chosen. No doubt there are characteristics which a would-be charismatic leader *must* exhibit to his or her audience of potential followers. If driven by a sense of personal incapacity, any audience surely will require that the leader appear to be able to solve the problems that its members cannot. The creation of such an appearance, especially when the audience is huge, may require great drama if it is to be persuasive. This in turn suggests that the would-be leader needs to possess rhetorical skills of a high order (and must have suitable ways of communicating with the masses).

It goes without saying that the would-be leader must project an aura of knowledge, strength, and effectiveness—traits rather like those expected of preferred political leaders in general.[47] But the question of how much objective evidence of capacity is needed remains. The answer is uncertain and likely to be quite variable because of the foibles of the human inference process. Students of

decision making find that information is often weighted in proportion to vividness rather than reliability.[48] Hence, it may be that little
solid evidence will be needed, and that the signals picked up by the
audience in assessing the would-be leader are sufficiently powerful
(though in objective terms nearly chimerical) to drive inferences
which in turn cement the bond. Once followers have embraced a
leader, their perception of his or her performances—often of wholly
ambiguous content and effect—are likely to be biased in the leader's
favor.[49] Summarizing the literature on impression formation, Roger
Brown[50] points out that in forming opinions of relevant others,
one goes beyond the available information, inferring the unknown
in a manner which is consistent with the initial impression. A very
positive initial impression can yield further attributions of a
strongly positive kind. As these attributions build, contrary evidence becomes progressively less able to penetrate the follower's
perspective.

Beyond the ability to send a dramatic and positive impression of
capacity, then, it is not clear that any truly singular features are
needed by an emergent charismatic leader. In this respect, being
chosen seems to depend substantially on being in the right place at
the right time. The seekers find their proxy, rather than the other
way around.

This does not mean that the bond is built entirely upon illusion;
even true believers require some real evidence that a leader can act
effectively in their behalf. Nor does it mean that a leader inevitably
must emerge; deteriorating conditions and hunger for salvation may
set the stage, but only if a visible player is able to broadcast the
right impression at the right time will bonding occur.

Self-efficacy theory also does not explain how a charismatic bond,
once formed, changes with time and circumstance. As discussed
earlier, falling back on proxy control—or, put differently, bonding
with a leader—has as its crucial effect the lowering of stress levels
and the provision of reassurance. It is the reduction of stress which
undergirds the fervor of commitment, a definitive element of charisma. For the follower the bond is made strong in proportion to
the relief experienced. But as time goes by, with stress reduced, will

the bond itself gradually be weakened as a consequence? Will the followers come to believe once again in their own coping abilities, and with self-efficacy restored, will a proxy no longer be needed? Or, alternatively, will a different kind of leadership be needed?

It may well be that charismatic bonding is an event which, especially for the young, carries formative significance. The whole experience may involve a sort of "imprinting" which is all but irreversible. Some survey studies show that searing political events can have such an impact on the young, leaving those swept up in such events indelibly marked and resistant to the influence of subsequent political developments.[51] Under those conditions, not even a rather full restoration of perceived self-efficacy would necessarily undermine commitment to the leader—although some of the psychological features of that commitment might change.

The Evolution of the Charismatic Bond

There is no research literature which specifies how a charismatic bond (or proxy control more generally) will evolve. However, with respect to the case of primary interest here—that is, the case of political charisma where the leader is bonded with a very large following—some theoretical guidance can be found in two bodies of research: that on complex organizations[52] and that on social/political identification.[53] The former is germane because the emergence of macroscopic political charisma generally will be followed by organization—and much more than minimal organization if the leader becomes the head of a government. The latter is germane because political charisma, when it takes root, can orient the attitudes and behaviors of the masses it affects for many years, making the cleavage between them and their opponents the primary basis for all of their political actions. And if this charisma extends nationwide, it can put in place a cleavage structure which drives the politics of the nation long after the leader has left.

Weber theorized that wholly unorganized ("pure") charisma would be short-lived in the macroscopic case, because as a mass phenomenon it soon must give way to the encroachments of rational organization through a process of "routinization." But if the period of pure charisma is brief, it nonetheless can be a time of searing reorientation for those in the mass following. A collection of despairing individuals is being forged into a community. At the outset, most of these individuals are linked only in that each is bonded with the leader. Soon the phenomenon becomes social, however, and the followers' recognition of this collective aspect (especially if given dramatic visibility in a mass congregation) brings solidarity of the type expected of "in-groups" in competitive environments. Some sequelae to this crystallization of in-group sentiment are well known: internal demands for loyalty and conformity, increased internal communication and interaction, enhanced hostility toward rivals, and distortion of perception to put the actions and characteristics of the in-group in the best possible light.[54]

Like all ethnocentrism, that which accompanies this new self-definition is driven by the need for positive self-esteem[55]—a need no doubt keenly felt where self-efficacy on matters of fundamental importance appears to have collapsed. What is especially important here is that the emergence of this in-group sentiment actually seems to work: Henri Tajfel and his collaborators[56] present evidence that the development of ethnocentrism does in fact enhance positive self-esteem. Thus, such a development in the charismatic bonding process provides additional reinforcement of those bonds and that identification. The adoption by the mass following of a self-conscious social/political identification is itself rewarding. This development surely adds considerable strength to the movement and drives the attendant us-versus-them cleavage deeper into the political culture.

The breadth of the charismatic reorientation of a population figures prominently in determining its staying power. If the followers represent a large enough portion of the population, the politics of the entire nation must change. Its cleavage structure will shift to fit the new realities, and this structure will remain in place until the passion of the followers, or more likely, of their generational replacements, has ebbed. (As the American New Dealers found, it is very difficult to hand down passionate commitment

through more than a generation or two when the social and economic conditions which gave rise to that commitment are no longer
in place.)

Another important factor in the ultimate staying power of the
charismatic reorientation is the evolution of form, as the bonding
between leader and mass becomes routinized. At the most general
level, routinization involves the gradual transformation of charisma
from a direct, concentrated, and emotionally intense relationship to
an indirect, dispersed, and less passionate one. Edward Shils[57] aptly
describes this as the "attenuation" of charisma.

Routinization's First Stage: The Development of Structure

Although Weber did not specify the steps in routinization, it seems
clear that two empirically separable developments may be anticipated. The first is mediation of the leader-to-mass flow of communications and benefits as certain key disciples gradually meta-
morphose into the lieutenants and high priests of the movement—
trusted agents who act in behalf of the leader. The emergence of
such intermediary roles, a development of fundamental importance
yet mundane appearance, occurs gradually as the leader finds it
more and more difficult to maintain frequent and direct ties with
his or her following. It is a development which flows from success,
from the need to deal with a large and scattered movement. With
such a transformation, and especially if the charismatic leader
becomes head of state, the ability of any such leader to maintain a
direct tie with his or her following is very much diminished.

As direct contact with the leader becomes occasional, the role of
intermediaries grows accordingly. It is true that those who initially
fill the intervening roles may sincerely wish to act only as carriers
of the faith, but sooner or later they cannot avoid becoming its
interpreters. Points of ambiguity or uncertainty about the leader's
views will arise; doctrinal messages will need amplification or clarification; routine questions will be put by the followers. And in
meeting the requirements of the situations they face, these intermediaries become more than mere conduits through which mes-

sages are passed. They interpret pronouncements; they fill doctrinal voids; they emphasize passages. In so doing, they inevitably begin to put something of their own perspectives, their own ideas, and their own values into the mix. Especially in an ideologically vacuous movement, but also in one in which the leader's views are well elaborated and even written down, there is little choice. Too much remains unclear and unspecified; too many situations are of uncertain meaning and implication. It is unavoidable that intermediaries come to shape the leader's message.

There also will be figures in the movement who gravitate to the leader on a more calculating basis, would-be lieutenants who see in the leader's success an opportunity for the advancement of themselves and their special interests. Unless this relationship has an important symbiotic element, the leader no doubt will wish to purge the movement of such figures. However, the crucial fact is that even when such self-interested actors are effectively eliminated (no simple task), intermediary roles will grow progressively more important to the functioning of the charismatic movement.

This first stage in the routinization of charisma, then, involves the appearance of intermediary roles between the leader and the mass of followers, a process which can be summarized as the development of structure. And, again, it must be emphasized that this development requires no assumption of betrayal or great personal ambition on the part of those who fill such roles. They may wish to be wholly faithful to the leader's doctrine and mission; they may wish to do only the leader's bidding. However, even in well-structured organizations, doctrine and mission can be subject to widely varying interpretations and understandings. In amorphous, large charismatic movements such uncertainties are sure to be increased dramatically. Hence the intermediaries must play active and discretionary parts in the functioning of such movements.

The development of structure inevitably and irresistibly carries with it an erosion of control at the center of the charismatic movement. The rapidity and extent of this process will depend on several interrelated factors. One already mentioned is the size and geographic distribution of the social aggregate involved, which has a direct bearing on the need for intermediaries. A second is the presence or absence of mass communication channels through which a leader can maintain regular and direct contact with the masses. And the third, perhaps less obvious in its implications than the others, is the rate and variability of environmental change. When change comes quickly and unpredictably on the political landscape, there may be little time available for peripherally located representatives to pass crucial information to, and receive policy directives from, the center of the movement. Adaptive problem solving often must be left in the hands of agents on the scene.

That central control will slip away under these conditions—that is, where a collective enterprise is very large, widely scattered, not well connected by direct communications networks, and subject to a rapidly changing environment—is an argument familiar to those who study organizations in general. In organization theory, however, the discussion is cast in terms of centralization and decentralization, which are themselves tied to the problems of information and control. Richard Cyert and Kenneth MacCrimmon write, for example:

> As an organization grows larger, it becomes more difficult for its management to maintain control. . . . The diseconomies and constraints on centralization take several primary forms. The fact that communication costs are higher for centralized structures suggests one advantage of decentralization. Furthermore, the recognition that individuals, especially those holding central control, have only a limited information-processing capacity indicates a natural pressure toward decentralization. . . . And if the environment is a friendly one, one from which the organization can draw support, decentralization may seem safe and desirable.[58]

Decentralization may seem safe and desirable, true, but in some situations that is beside the point: decentralization is unavoidable. Full control cannot be retained at the center, for example, in a rapidly changing military conflict. Subordinate units directly involved in battlefield activities must—and will—adapt as best they can. Or in a more conventionally political example, control over the waging of an electoral campaign across a large geographic expanse must be shared with what Dwaine Marvick calls "outpost personnel." He writes:

> Outpost personnel are indispensable to partisan campaign efforts . . . and they possess certain residual controls over how the campaign is waged. It is up to the active partisans and enthusiasts to carry the message into lukewarm or even hostile quarters. They personalize the standardized campaign appeals emanating from headquarters. . . . They convey not only the basic message (so far as they understand the desired emphasis) but they also add their own ideological and/or ethical comments by word or gesture. . . . The most important point about these outpost activists is that they are able, in a face-to-face situation, to make spontaneous field corrections in the political communication process. They are on the scene. . . . [But] they are not neutral instruments.[59]

Decentralization may be required by the environment, but it also may be required by the enormity of the job facing the leader. Hugh Heclo comments on the illusory nature of centralized control in the U.S. presidency: "Presidential government is an illusion—an illusion misleads presidents no less than the media and the American public. . . . Presidential government is the idea that the president . . . is or can be in charge of governing the country. This is an 'illusion' in the fullest sense of the word, for it is based on appearances that mislead and deceive. . . . Far from being in charge or running the government, the president must struggle even to comprehend what is going on."[60]

In sum, large charismatic movements, if they are to survive for an extended period, will inevitably develop structure and with that structure will come some decentralization of influence. These changes will be compounded if the movement's leader takes on the burdens inherent in being head of government. And although it is true that slippage of control may be slowed by the uniquely worshipful and adoring stance taken by early intermediaries toward the leader, it cannot be stopped, even with such devotion.

Routinization's Second Stage: Dispersion of the Charismatic Response

The second and more mysterious step in the routinization of charisma is the dispersion of the charismatic response. The flow of responses from following to leader—an amalgam of what Lasswell called empowering responses and, more peculiar to charisma, emotional fervor—gradually begins to change shape with the appearance of intermediaries in the stream. Eventually some of these secondary figures come (perhaps inadvertently) to share in, and in rare instances may even come to monopolize, the aura of power and effectiveness upon which the attachment to the leader depends. In other words, in the course of everyday performance of their roles, some intermediaries come to be seen as themselves very special. Initially they are honored only as the agents of the leader, but over time they gradually acquire a somewhat more independent claim to the attentions of the following or of one of its segments.

Weber touched somewhat ambiguously on this feature of routinization in discussing the development of a "charisma of office." Shils gives it greater attention. Writing of the response of the followers to the intermediary actor, he comments: "What the [follower] responds to is not just the specific declaration or order of the incumbent in the role . . . but the incumbent enveloped in the vague and powerful nimbus of the authority of the entire institution. It is a legitimacy constituted by sharing the properties of the 'organization as a whole' *epitomized or symbolized in the powers concentrated (or thought to be concentrated) at the peak.* This is 'institutional' charisma."[61]

We can find no empirical evidence which might be used to set expectations with respect to the parameters of this psychological process. And we cannot be sure how divided loyalties might square with the need for proxy control over important events. It may be that the successful charismatic leader—that is, the leader who seems to have successfully coped with the crisis which undermined the followers' self-efficacy—will experience a weakening of the bond with those followers. In a sense, it might be argued, the followers have recovered from their affliction. They can then psychologically afford to be more devoted to the less imposing but more proximal figures in the movement, the intermediaries who deal with the "bread and butter" issues of everyday life.

Or the change may occur for another reason; dispersion of influence may be especially likely for the *un*successful charismatic leader who, though empowered, ultimately cannot solve the problems of the erstwhile adoring masses. The movement may be held together by the inherent attractions of social/political in-group identification and the continued ethnocentrism it permits. But though the movement is still present, it will have changed its shape.

In the end, there is no reason to suppose that all followers will see the leader, the organizational intermediaries, or the evolving situation in the same way. For some, the end of their personal crises and the restoration of a sense of efficacy will come more quickly. For others, it will not come at all. For some, the intermediary figures will be embraced as new leaders. For others, they are unimportant. For some, the original bond will remain passionate and strong. For others, it will erode. It surely would be wrong to argue that followers will change simultaneously or uniformly.

Of the many factors which influence the evolution of a charismatic bond, none is more important than the capacity of the leader to control the institutional apparatus—the central problem of all governance. Establishment of information and control systems may be useful. Another important technique is to rotate key personnel from job to job, making them less likely to acquire personal followings. But even the most brilliant defense of mission and power can do no more than slow the process whereby some elements of the following slip away from the leader's domination. Sooner or later the content of the charismatic bond will subtly shift for more and more followers as what had been a simple relationship with the leader becomes, over time, a complex one with the leader and individual deputies. Indeed, even before the leader's death or displacement, it is not impossible that in some instances and for some followers the shift will ultimately be complete, with the deputies rather than the leader held to be at the heart of the movement.

In sum, a dispersion of the following's charismatic response will depend upon many factors. Likely to be especially important are the nature and extent of the contact between its members and those figures of the organizational apparatus. Secondary personnel who come to be seen as relatively independent sources of benefits are the most likely to acquire their own supporters. And this will be true whether or not such supporters are actually encouraged. Even the most conscientious and loyal lieutenant may be cast into the limelight and appear to be an important source of benefits for segments of the following. All in all, it is very likely that in the long run the organization will come to dominate the day-to-day relationship with followers, even though the leader remains a central focus for emotional ties.

This does not mean that the dispersion of the charismatic response—or in Shils's terms, the growth of institutional charisma —inevitably will become sufficient to guarantee the cohesion or even the continuance of the movement when the leader's time at center stage ends. Succession is a special problem, and examples of (presumably) charismatic leaders whose missions died with them are common. However, as noted earlier, a charismatic movement which has reoriented the cleavage structure of a nation is likely to continue in one form or another. If the conditions which created the widespread collapse in self-efficacy are still in place, the movement may simply gain a new leader. If those conditions have eased, institutionalization may continue but with more the coloring of a political party than that of a fervent mass movement. Under these conditions, and especially when the original charismatic movement lacked ideological content, the direction taken by the organization will depend upon its current leadership. If that leadership must vie for power in an electoral context, it seems likely sooner or later to become entrepreneurial, less concerned with the views of the original leader than with the need for victory—though the new leadership's policies, whatever they are, will no doubt be justified in terms of the original leader's wishes. Such entrepreneurial leadership probably accelerates change in the socioeconomic underpinnings of the movement or party.

Studying Political Charisma

Many fascinating and important phenomena in political life, though in principle available for empirical study, in practice present intractable problems to the would-be systematic investigator. As a result these phenomena are left in a condition of scientific limbo sometimes described as theory rich but data poor. Political charisma is one such phenomenon, and it is no surprise that its empirical study is in its infancy. This is in part due to the definitional swamp in which the subject has been mired. However, it is also attributable to the seemingly impossible problems faced by any would-be systematic investigator. Consider what a really good research design should entail. Given the fact that charisma is an influence relationship, data must come from both sides of that relationship. Thus, something must be known of the leader and his or her behavior. And much, much more must be known of the followers and the bases of their receptivity to the leader's appeal. What is more, these data must not be collected at only a single point in time. Charisma is a dynamic phenomenon, developing and evolving as a response to changing circumstances and at different rates in different sectors of the relevant population. The leader's appeal will be shaped by the changing context in which that appeal is offered. In other words, with respect to the time of emergence of charisma and, equally, with respect to its evolution, data must be obtained which describe both leader and following as they move through changing times. Finally, the observations of individuals should be supplemented by data describing the context. The meaning of societal crisis must be given objective as well as perceptual definition.

It goes without saying that no such research design has ever been employed. The issue of timing, alone, presents insuperable difficulties. The emergence of the charismatic bond is a process for which there is no advance notice. No doubt it begins subtly and gradually, as a crisis primes its victims for leadership and as some figure starts to advance—at least in the eyes of a significant group of those victims—to center stage. To be ready to capture such a development in micro-level data would be miraculous. Indeed, to be ready to collect such observations even when the crisis response in the mass public is in full swing, as might be the case in a massive general rally for the leader, would be almost unprecedented in public attitude research. It is true that interesting "street" observations can be made in such a setting—and we make use of some of them here—but though illustrative and sometimes fascinating, such unsystematic evidence will never be adequate to explain charismatic bonding and evolution.

Some contextual data often can be collected from official sources well after the fact. But perceptual data from the individuals caught up in a charismatic experience is of even more uncertain reliability if its origin is not in the time period of its focus. And then there are the problems always associated with collecting survey data in highly charged political contexts where suspicions run high and assumptions about social research are distinctly negative.

In the face of all of these problems, one option is simply to give up on macroscopic studies which treat "real world" events and to settle for microscopic analogues which are more manageable. But though small group experiments have much to recommend them, in this particular case questions of external validity loom large. For example, both the role of social facilitation in the following's response and the importance of extended crisis in the decay of self-efficacy are extremely difficult to capture, even in silhouette, in a small group study. Moreover, political scientists interested in charisma are concerned not just with its psychological roots but also with its larger implications for governance and for societal evolution. Given these considerations, empirical study of political charisma in the real world is greatly to be desired.

It can be no surprise to learn that the present study relies upon a body of empirical evidence which is far from the ideal. Nonetheless, we believe it to be suited—indeed, given the present state of research on political charisma, uniquely suited—to the task. Individual-level data are blended with multiple levels of aggregate data to construct a picture which, if not wholly verified, is still well supported by the evidence. And the evidence is striking not because it alone is conclusive, but because it fits so well with the other kinds of results reviewed in this chapter. In the absence of such a fit the findings presented below would obviously be less impressive.

This study takes as its empirical focus the case of Juan Perón and his Peronistas. The setting is Argentina, in a period bounded by the near collapse of its agricultural economy in the early 1940s and the return of Perón to power, in 1973, after eighteen years of exile. This is not an Argentine story, however. The leader and followers were of that country, but the story deals with charisma in general, and the evidence speaks less to questions of Argentine politics than to the development and evolution of charismatic bonds. Our purpose here is theoretical, focusing on a phenomenon which is general to humanity rather than peculiar to a nation.

Four chapters follow this one. In Chapter 2 the Peronist case is put into broader context. After a sketch of pertinent features of Argentine history, the circumstances immediately preceding the emergence of Perón as a political actor of consequence and then as a charismatic figure are detailed. Special attention is given to dramatic changes in the economic and social landscapes. Journalistic accounts are used to provide first-hand descriptions of the events surrounding Perón's move to center stage in Argentine politics. The chapter continues with a discussion of his initial terms as president (1946–1955), his period of exile and the changes in Peronism which occurred in that period (1955–1973), and finally his return to power in 1973 and his death the following year.

Chapter 3 presents aggregate data studies of Perón's first electoral success, in 1946. This election came in a period of crisis in Argentine politics—which, in turn, came after a more prolonged period of crisis in the country's rural economy. The aggregate data studies cannot substitute for the type of survey-based perceptual and demographic studies which would have provided a definitive portrait of Perón's true believers. The aggregate data can be used, however, to make strong inferences about certain demographic features of his following. The methodological pitfalls of such analyses are discussed.

Chapter 4 deals with the routinization of charisma. The research draws upon data from a national survey taken almost exactly midway between Perón's expulsion from Argentina and his triumphant return. This serendipitously timed set of observations permits an empirical examination of Peronism twenty years after its inception. Two forms of Peronism are identified, one tied to the man himself and the other tied to the movement. Social and psychological bases for these separate orientations are identified, and their interrelationship modeled. Finally, the recruitment processes feeding each wing of Peronism are explored.

Chapter 5 examines the development of Peronism subsequent to the death of its leader, summarizes the research findings, and offers some remarks on the creation and evolution of a charismatic bond.

★ 2 ★

Peronism: Its Context and Evolution

Juan Domingo Perón emerged from relative obscurity into the center of Argentine politics in July 1943, as one of a group of field-grade army officers who carried out a military coup. Before turning to the train of events subsequent to the coup and the evolution of the Peronist phenomenon, let us look briefly at the broader political and economic context in which those developments occurred.

Pre-Perón Argentina

After attaining independence from Spain in 1819, Argentina was characterized by chaos and anarchy for almost a half century. For most of this period there was no national government, and in local areas if order existed it was forcibly imposed by a *caudillo,* or strongman. Argentina as a nation-state did not exist. Then, in 1861, the army of Buenos Aires decisively defeated the army of the interior provinces, and the next year Bartolomé Mitre, the governor of Buenos Aires, became Argentina's first truly national president.

Mitre and his first two successors concentrated their efforts on pacification of the country and creation of the institutions of government. The Congress was moved to Buenos Aires and began to meet regularly; a national judiciary was created and staffed with people noted for their competence, rather than for their political loyalties.[1] The city of Buenos Aires was removed from the province of that name and converted into a federal district (which we refer to as the Federal Capital, to avoid confusion with the province), much like Washington, D.C. And, most important, general acceptance was gained for the existence of a national government.

Beginning in 1880, emphasis shifted from political foundations to economic development. At that time there were a million and a half Argentines, most of whom were engaged in subsistence agriculture, occupying about a million square miles of territory. Turn-of-the-century administrations set out to change this by importing from Europe both labor and capital. The rail system, owned by the British, was rapidly enlarged from 2,000 miles of track to 20,000.[2] The amount of cultivated land was increased from less than 1.5 million acres in 1872 to more than 25 million in 1914,[3] and the amount of land devoted to grazing was increased almost as much. These and similar factors changed Argentina from a subsistence agricultural system to a major exporter of primary products. By the time of World War I, Argentina was exporting 350,000 tons of beef and 5 million tons of cereals annually.

At the same time Argentina was also importing European settlers. The principal framer of the constitution had said "To govern is to populate," and this dictum was taken to heart by the nation's nineteenth-century rulers. Their efforts to attract Europeans to Argentina proved quite successful. Immigration began in the 1850s as little more than a trickle but increased rapidly during the next forty years. In 1870, 40,000 immigrants arrived; in 1885, 110,000; and in 1890, 200,000.[4] Many of these immigrants came only to harvest crops and then returned to their homelands, primarily Italy and Spain, but enough remained that between 1869 and 1929 60 percent of Argentina's population growth came from immigration.[5] In proportional terms, immigration to Argentina was appreciably greater than to the United States at about the same time (see Figure 2.1).

The immigrants to Argentina differed in at least one important way from their North American counterparts: they did not become citizens. In spite of the relative simplicity of the naturalization process, as of 1895 only 0.16 percent had been naturalized; nineteen years later the figure was still only 1.4 percent.[6] This lack of citizenship, plus the weakness of the trade union movement, meant that the long-term political mobilization of immigrants was difficult.

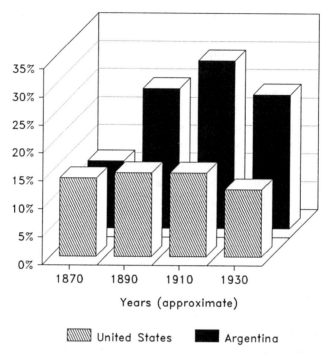

Figure 2.1 Immigrants as a percentage of total population in the United
States and Argentina. Source: Oscar Cornblit, "Inmigrantes y
empresarios en la política argentina," in Torcuato DiTella and
Tulio Halperín Donghi, eds., *Los fragmentos del poder* (Buenos
Aires: Jorge Alvarez, 1969), p. 394.

Rapid economic development during the last quarter of the nine-
teenth century allowed a great many Argentines to attain a substantial degree of well-being. By the time of World War I the
standard of living in Argentina was much higher than elsewhere in
Latin America and comparable to that of southern Europe. This
economic development, however, was not accompanied by a similar
level of political development; most Argentines remained almost
completely removed from the political process. Several political
parties existed, but until 1890 all were essentially conservative organizations representing different sectors of the aristocracy—primarily

the large landowners of the interior and the commercial and live-stock interests of the city and province of Buenos Aires.

This political system worked reasonably well during the nation's formative years, when its social structure was composed almost exclusively of a small landowning elite and a large, politically inarticulate mass. The system did not work as well when the social structure underwent fundamental alteration. The most obvious feature of that change was the rapid formation of a middle class, composed largely of immigrants and their offspring. Ysabel Rennie says of these immigrants: "They took up land, they opened small shops, they bought property, they saved their money. By the end of the century they were the most stable element in the community. . . . In commerce and industry foreigners outnumbered criollos three to one. . . . In medicine they outnumbered Argentine doctors five to one. They predominated in the construction industry, in transport, in whatever was not the care and feeding of cows and the harvesting of crops. . . . The immigrants were the middle class."[7]

It was this new middle class that formed the base for the nation's first major nonaristocratic political party, the Radical Civic Union (UCR), founded in 1890. During the first forty years of its existence, this party was dominated by a single enigmatic politician, Hipólito Yrigoyen. Convinced that UCR participation in elections supervised by the Conservatives would only serve to place the party's stamp of approval on inevitable electoral fraud, Yrigoyen saw to it that the Radicals boycotted all elections prior to 1912. Instead, they attempted to come to power by force, instigating rebellions in 1890, 1893, and 1905. When these revolts proved unsuccessful, the Radicals still did not nominate candidates for office or write specific programs; they seemed content with denunciations of the oligarchic nature of the government and insisted that it be replaced by a "national renovation."

In an effort to bring more people to the polls and thus increase the legitimacy of the regime, the Conservatives in 1911 wrote a new election law. The law provided for universal and compulsory male suffrage, a secret ballot, permanent voter registration, and minority representation in the Congress. The Conservatives felt able to enact universal manhood suffrage because such a large part of the urban working class was composed of foreigners.[8] Even under the new law, manual workers, artisans, and small merchants were quite underrepresented in the electorate, while white-collar workers, and especially professionals, were dramatically overrepresented (see Table 2.1).

Within five years, the honest administration of this law cost the Conservatives their monopoly on public office. In 1916, in what was probably the nation's first open competitive presidential election, Hipólito Yrigoyen became Argentina's first non-Conservative president. Unfortunately, the Radicals, still lacking a concrete program, seemed to have no idea how to put into effect the "national renovation" they had been promising for a quarter century. They held power for fourteen years but, in spite of some reforms in education and health, attempted no fundamental change, and the economic power of the Conservatives remained intact. It seems that by this time the Radicals had lost their revolutionary zeal, if indeed such zeal had ever existed. Their goal appears to have become simply recognition of the right of the middle class to participate fully in

Table 2.1 Occupational breakdown of the labor force (1914) and the electorate (1918) in the Federal Capital (in percent).

Occupation	Labor Force	Electorate
Manual workers	31.1	22.2
Artisans and small merchants	35.6	28.8
Employees	17.9	30.1
Owners	2.8	2.9
Professionals	6.5	14.4
Other	6.1	1.6

Source: Richard Walter, *The Socialist Party of Argentina, 1890–1930* (Austin: University of Texas Press, 1977), pp. 125, 239.

the economic, social, and political life of the country—and, at least for Radical leaders, the right to a share in the spoils of office.

In 1912 the Conservatives had been willing to *share* power with the Radicals, although certainly not on the basis of equality. They saw the provision in the new election law guaranteeing minority representation in Congress as a means of coopting their middle-class opponents. (The congressional debate on the law makes it clear that the Conservatives did not envision the possibility that they could become the minority party.) What the Conservatives were unwilling to do was to *relinquish* power to the Radicals, yet this is what happened. Voter participation increased from 190,000 in 1910 to 640,000 in 1912 and 1,460,000 in 1928, a growth of more than 750 percent in less than two decades. And as the electorate increased in size so did the percentage of the vote obtained by the Radicals. Equally alarming to the Conservatives must have been the fact that the Radicals, who appear to have held little appeal for the urban working class in 1916, fared quite well in working-class areas in 1928. (In 1916, in the twenty wards of the Federal Capital the rank order correlation between the percentage of the registered voters who were manual workers and the percentage of the vote received by the UCR was −.81; in 1928 that correlation was +.54.) In Figure 2.2 one can see that in the Federal Capital between 1916 and 1928 the percentage of the vote received by Radical candidates increased in nine of the ten wards with the largest percentage of manual workers, while it declined in all ten of the wards with the lowest percentage of workers.

In September 1930 the disastrous effects of the world depression, ever-increasing corruption in the government, the senility of President Yrigoyen (who was serving a second term), recognition by the Conservatives that the rules of the game had to be changed if they were to return to power, and widespread popular disillusionment with the Radicals led to their overthrow and the establishment of Argentina's first military government.[9]

The 1930 coup marked the beginning of a new era in Argentina. The preceding seventy years had been characterized by a degree of political stability almost unknown in Latin America and by a level

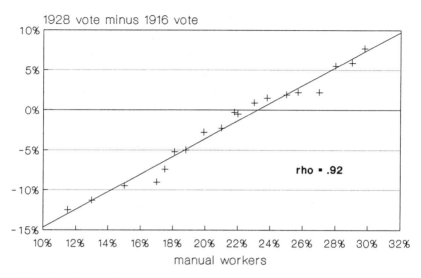

Figure 2.2 Change in the Radical vote in the Federal Capital by percentage of manual workers. Source: Richard J. Walter, *The Socialist Party of Argentina, 1890–1930* (Austin: University of Texas Press, 1977), pp. 139, 215, 237.

of economic development that substantially raised the standard of living of many Argentines. The years following 1930, in contrast, have been characterized by exactly the opposite: economic stagnation and an extraordinary degree of political instability.

Within two years the Argentine armed forces returned power to the Conservatives by means of elections as fraudulent as those held prior to 1911. This second period of Conservative rule is referred to by Argentine historians as the Era of Patriotic Fraud, for according to the Conservatives it was their patriotic duty to engage in electoral fraud in order to make sure that the Radicals did not hoodwink the immature voters and once again lead the country down the road to ruin.[10]

The elite forces that governed Argentina prior to 1916 had been dedicated to national development. Such commitment was decidedly not characteristic of the elite which came to power following the 1930 coup. They did lead the nation out of the depression and restore a degree of national prosperity; however, they also saw to it that this prosperity was distributed even more inequitably than before. Argentina was run almost exclusively for the benefit of the landed aristocracy.

During this second conservative period (1931–1943) there occurred a profound change in the character of the urban working class. At the time of World War I, a majority of the workers in the cities were recent European immigrants—in the Federal Capital more than 80 percent of the manual workers fourteen years of age and older were foreigners.[11] But by the time of World War II, workers were primarily recent migrants from the countryside and, to a lesser extent, the children of immigrants.

In Argentina, as elsewhere, rural to urban migration was a result both of push from the countryside and of pull from the cities. Each of these was, to some extent, a result of the world depression and of World War II. The former had devastating effects on agricultural exporters such as Argentina. Agricultural production, especially in cereals, declined precipitously. For example, between 1937 and 1947 the amount of land planted in wheat and corn declined by 36.5 percent,[12] with most of that land being put into pasture—which required many fewer workers. This meant that a great many renters, sharecroppers and day laborers were quite literally pushed out of the countryside. At the same time the depression, and later the war, forced Argentina to accelerate its rate of industrialization, thus increasing the attraction of the cities, where employment opportunities were believed to be greater.

The changing contribution of agriculture and industry to Argentina's gross domestic product during the 1935–1946 period can be seen in Figure 2.3. Although the contribution of agriculture fluctuates appreciably from year to year, the trend clearly is one of decline, especially after 1941. The contribution of industry, in contrast, increased almost constantly, though not dramatically.

During the late 1930s and early 1940s migration from rural areas to the cities reached exceptional proportions. It is estimated that in a single four-year period, 1943–1947, one out of every five rural dwellers moved to an urban center.[13] Most moved to greater Buenos

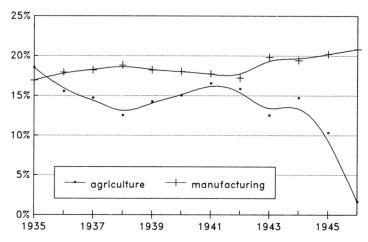

Figure 2.3 Contributions of agriculture and manufacturing to gross
   domestic product, 1935–1946. Source: Carlos Díaz Alejandro,
   Essays on the Economic History of the Argentine Republic (New
   Haven: Yale University Press, 1970), Appendix.

Aires. Germani estimated that by 1947 almost three-fourths of the
working class in greater Buenos Aires was composed of migrants
from the interior provinces.[14]

The European immigrants who had formed the bulk of the urban
working class during the early twentieth century brought with them
political ideologies such as anarchism, syndicalism, and anarcho-
syndicalism. The internal migrants, however, had no such ideological baggage. Life in the countryside, whether as an agricultural
laborer or as a tenant farmer, had been very hard, but it had been
relatively predictable. The patron-client relationship meant that
hard work and absolute loyalty to one's boss led to at least a degree
of security. Life in the large cities was quite different. There were
movies and sidewalk cafés, but there was no *patrón*. Trade unions
were available almost exclusively to skilled workers; the owners of
slaughterhouses and packing plants, where the more fortunate
migrants found employment, had successfully fought against unionization. And many migrants had difficulty finding work of any sort.

One difference between the new urban working class and its

earlier counterpart was most significant: its members were citizens and hence potential voters. Argentine political institutions were not equipped to handle a massive increase in political participation. Neither the structures, nor the programs, nor the leaders of the existing political parties offered anything of value to this new working class. Until 1940 the Congress was dominated by the Conservatives, who seemed totally uninterested in the plight of the workers. For the next three years, the Radicals used their congressional majority almost exclusively to harass the Conservative president and to prevent the enactment of any sort of program. The recent arrivals from the countryside appeared to receive attention only from the Socialists, and they had at least two strikes against them. The Socialists had managed to elect a few congressmen and city council members, but these representatives had been unable to improve the miserable conditions of the urban workers. More important, perhaps, in the Socialists' failure to rally many workers to their cause, was that they tried to appeal to the migrants with what must have seemed like unintelligible ideas. The migrants almost certainly were more interested in a new *patrón* than in Karl Marx. In the countryside they had been accustomed to following individuals, not abstract ideas.

Peronist Argentina

In 1943 the armed forces once again became the keeper of the national conscience and deposed the Conservative government. The 1943 coup was organized and led by a group of field-grade army officers united in a military lodge called the Group of United Officers (GOU). One of its leaders was a colonel who was to change the very nature of Argentine politics: Juan Domingo Perón. Immediately following the coup, Perón was appointed under-secretary of war. Four months later he added what turned out to be the key post in his rise to power: secretary of labor. As soon as he gained the latter office he began an active campaign for working-class support. He saw to it that wages were increased substantially and that ameliorative labor legislation was enforced—much of it for the first time. He presided over the formation of new trade unions and the expansion of those existing unions that were friendly toward him. Under his influence, for example, membership in the Textile Workers Union went from about 2,000 in 1943 to more than 84,000 in 1946; the Metallurgical Workers Union grew from 2,000 to 100,000 during the same period.[15] By 1945 his Labor Secretariat was the nation's sole collective bargaining agency, and under its auspices unions were virtually certain to obtain whatever they sought.

Nominal wage rates for urban workers increased significantly while Perón headed the Labor Secretariat, later the Labor Ministry.[16] Although it is true that much of this increase was eroded by inflation, real wages increased by 12 percent, and it may well be that the increase in nominal wages was the more important. One can imagine that Perón's followers gave him full credit for the nominal increases while blaming some mysterious other factor for the inflation that devoured much of this increase.

Perón went to great lengths to dramatize each move and to obtain widespread publicity for his pro-labor stance. In his public speeches he identified with the throngs of listening workers: "You're dirty and I'm dirty. We're dirty together."[17] He walked among and drank with the workers of the industrial suburbs of the Federal Capital, and this image was carried to a wider audience by his future wife's popular radio program, "Toward a Better Future," which portrayed Perón as the Latin Superman.[18]

The Formation of the Bond

Perón's undertakings while in the Labor Ministry may have been sufficient to gain him a large following, but deeds alone are never sufficient for the formation of a charismatic bond. Rhetoric and dramatic actions count for little unless there is a receptive audience. As discussed in Chapter 1, crisis seems to be a necessary precondition for the emergence of a charismatic leader. And for many Argentines the early 1940s were certainly years of crisis.

The economic straits of the depression, which by 1940 had been

ameliorated for the large landowners and most wealthy busi-
nessmen, continued unabated into the mid-1940s for most of the
nation's poor. As already mentioned, economic collapse in the countryside prompted many of the rural poor to move to the nation's
cities. The problems for urban areas that had to absorb these
migrants were staggering. The already ample urban labor pool was
filled to the point of overflow, ensuring the continuance of depression wage rates. (From the depths of the depression until 1944
there was virtually no change in real urban wage rates.)[19] And, as
was to be expected, the new migrants typically moved into the labor
pool at its lowest level. In 1946 more than half of the working class
of greater Buenos Aires was composed of recent migrants; the
national census taken a year later showed that 75 percent of the
unskilled workers, 60 percent of the semi-skilled, and 50 percent
of the skilled workers of greater Buenos Aires were migrants.[20]

The influx of migrants also led to an acute housing shortage—
many, perhaps most, of those moving to the cities could find no
place to live. Shanty towns sprang up in all the nation's cities,
especially in the capital and its suburbs. Those from the countryside
were accustomed to building their own homes, but the cities offered
them no stones, trees, or the means of fashioning adobe. The new-
comers therefore worked with whatever was at hand—corrugated
tin, cardboard, even discarded automobile batteries. These shanty
towns, or *villas miserias,* were completely lacking in public services;
there were no streets, no electricity, and no running water.[21]

A second dimension of the crisis was political. The urban workers
of the early 1940s no longer resembled the unnaturalized and
apolitical workers of an earlier generation. With the Conservative
restoration in 1930 those members of the working class who had
begun to be politically engaged suddenly became unable to take
effective political action. For a while, they may have blamed the
newly hostile environment, but it is reasonable to suspect that at
some point during the 1930s or early 1940s many came to doubt
their ability to cope with their environment, and thus became
willing to accept, or perhaps even seek, proxy control. One would
expect this retreat to proxy control to have been even more wide-

spread among those newly arrived in the nation's cities. These migrants had left economic circumstances which had become intolerable, but they also left behind what earlier had been a degree of security and a sense of personal identity. Neither was available in their new urban environment. And the migrants from the countryside, accustomed to a patron-client relationship, were perhaps especially willing, even eager to accept proxy control.

It usually is difficult, if not impossible, to tie the bonding between a charismatic leader and his original followers to a particular event. The case of Juan Perón is thus exceptional in this respect. The magical event took place on the evening of October 17, 1945. By mid-1945 Perón was not only head of the Labor Ministry but also minister of war, head of the Post-War Council, and vice-president. He clearly was in the process of becoming the real power in the military government when, on October 9, he was arrested by a group of army officers who opposed both his political ambition and his pro-labor policies.

News of Perón's arrest was received with varying emotions by the leaders of the General Confederation of Labor (CGT, the Argentine equivalent of the AFL-CIO). Many labor leaders were impressed with his actions of the preceding two years, but others saw him in a quite different light: an army officer, therefore an enemy; an ambitious politician, not to be trusted; a friend only to those in the labor movement who would do his bidding. On October 16 the leaders of the CGT decided, after lengthy debate and a very narrow vote, to call a general strike to begin in two days. Citing the minutes of that meeting, David Tamarin[22] says that the leaders of the nation's organized labor movement were aware that they were being pulled along by rank-and-file workers who had already seized the initiative. The leader of the Meat Packers Union said, "If this body does not resolve to call a general strike let me assure you that it will be unable to contain the strike that will come from the volatile state of the workers. That is to say if we do not lead this movement it will happen anyway." His words were prophetic; by the time it was decided to call the general strike, tens of thousands of workers were already in the streets.[23]

The next day, October 17, at least 250,000 and perhaps as many as 500,000 people jammed into the Plaza de Mayo demanding the release of Perón.[24] The correspondent of the *Times* described the demonstration:

All of the personalism peculiar to Argentine politics, and the mystic fervor of the Argentine people reached a frenzied climax last night when Colonel Perón, looking weak and ill, addressed a crowd of several hundred thousand workers from the balcony of the Government House in the historic Plaza de Mayo. Before Colonel Perón appeared the crowd almost became hysterical with impatience and shouted "Where is he?" . . . The crowd was not preoccupied with ideologies or doctrines or programs, but wanted only Colonel Perón. . . . The crowd felt an almost religious emotion for Colonel Perón and not satisfied with having him as president, wanted to canonize him as well. On the walls was chalked "Saint Perón, President of Argentina."[25]

One of Argentina's foremost historians also has described the dramatic scene:

Thousands upon thousands of men and women from the suburban belt began to peacefully invade the center of the city [of Buenos Aires]. They shouted tirelessly the name of Perón, demanding his release. . . . This multitude searched instinctively for the Plaza de Mayo, the seat of power since the epoch of the Spaniards. There at the rose-colored Government House they were convinced that their single, obsessive grievance would be heeded. Growing by tens of thousands each hour, the masses were firmly ensconced in the historic plaza, shouting the name of their leader, becoming more and more impatient, and refusing to listen to anyone other than Perón. Finally, at almost midnight, Perón delivered an ambiguous, but vibrant speech, a speech interrupted constantly by a clamorous dialogue of love that *established, definitively, a bond between the leader and his people*.[26]

It is frequently forgotten that the events of October 17 were not limited to the Plaza de Mayo and the hundreds of thousands who witnessed Perón's return. Similar demonstrations, albeit on a smaller scale, took place in many provincial cities, and a great many people heard Perón's speech on the radio. Félix Luna says that the "millions who had their radios on shared the euphoria of their colleagues in the Plaza de Mayo."[27]

Luna also reminds us that October 17 was not immediately forgotten and replaced with business as usual. "The euphoria of triumph, the indescribable sensation of having been protagonists at an historical event and of having defeated the enemy, led the people to return to the Plaza de Mayo. Nobody worked on October 18th: there was no transportation, no banks, no movies, no public administration, no school, no industry and no business. This strike had nothing to do with the general strike declared earlier by the CGT; that Thursday there was a strike because those who had triumphed the day before needed to relive the certainty of that victory."[28]

Although it is clear when the charismatic bonding with the original followers took place, it is not clear how long the period of relatively pure or concentrated charisma lasted—through the time of Perón's election to the presidency in February 1946? Perhaps until the time of his inauguration, five months later?

For a full decade after the demonstration on October 17 (which soon came to be a national holiday, the Day of Loyalty) Juan Domingo Perón was the master of Argentina. Within a few days several union leaders announced the formation of a Labor Party, which almost immediately nominated Perón as its presidential candidate in the elections to be held the following February. Perón was opposed by a single candidate, José Tamborini of the UCR, who was supported by all other political parties, from the Communists to the Conservatives.

A pair of North American journalists who followed the election campaign wrote: "Perón's almost hypnotic powers were in evidence during his campaign for the presidency. In Rosario, women fainted by the dozens in a huge square where Perón was speaking, and girls of the bobby sox age chased his train as it moved slowly along the campaign route."[29] Of a speech given on February 12 during a strong rainstorm, Joseph Page says: "The charismatic attraction that Perón possessed now made its presence felt. It reached the thousands of people who were still seeking shelter under awnings, in doorways and against building walls. They scurried like ants to fill the empty spaces in the streets and sidewalks below the podium."[30]

During the brief campaign Perón attracted additional supporters with his adroit use of executive decrees. (Although he resigned his government positions before the campaign officially began, it was clear to all that the nation's president, General Edelmiro Farrell, was little more than a figurehead for Perón.) The executive decree thought to have been of greatest aid to Perón during the campaign was one issued on Christmas Eve, often referred to as the *aguinaldo* (Christmas present). This decree granted wage increases to everyone, except domestic servants and government employees, and provided an annual bonus equal to one month's pay.

In what even his opponents admitted was an honest election, Perón won with relative ease, obtaining about 1.5 million votes to his opponent's 1.2 million. Peronist candidates won almost 70 percent of the seats in the lower house of Congress and all but two Senate seats; they also gained the governorship and legislative majorities in every province except Corrientes. A detailed analysis of the socioeconomic bases of Perón's support in this election is the subject of Chapter 3.

Development of Structure

After his inauguration, Perón faced the necessity of delegating authority and responsibility, something he was quite reluctant to do throughout his political career. Perhaps he realized that the appointment of competent lieutenants would threaten his direct ties to his followers, or perhaps he simply mistrusted all those around him. In any event, the only person he entrusted with any appreciable authority was his wife, Evita, who in fact, though not in name, took control of the Labor Ministry. Before becoming president, Perón had been able to spend most of his time wooing the nation's workers, but after his inauguration that became impossible. Responsibility for maintaining working-class support was turned over to Evita, who not only maintained that support for her husband but broadened it. In addition to dealing with the organized working class, Evita appealed to the unorganized urban poor. She founded the Eva Perón Foundation, which soon swallowed up the nation's older charities. She spent huge sums to build hospitals and clinics and low-cost housing for the poor; she also held weekly audiences at which almost all petitioners were given whatever they needed.

We have noted that a charismatic bond cannot be maintained by illusion alone, and during Perón's first administration it certainly was not. Between 1946 and 1955 the working class benefited, both materially and psychologically. The process of unionization was continued,[31] wages and fringe benefits were increased, a modern social security system was created, and there was a dramatic redistribution of income favoring the working class.[32]

Perón also managed to attain virtually full employment, in part through the new jobs created via import substitution industrialization, and in part through padding the federal payroll. In the period between 1940 and 1944 government employees accounted for 6.6 percent of the economically active population; during the 1945–49 period that percentage increased to 8.8, and by 1950–54 to 9.3. Between 1942 and 1955 the economically active population increased by 38 percent, while the number of persons employed by the national government increased by 98 percent.[33]

Soon after his inauguration Perón built new homes for more than two million people.[34] These huge concrete apartment houses were ugly, but they were a vast improvement over the *villas miserias*.

Besides relying heavily upon Evita as his trusted agent, Perón also attempted to slow the natural tendency toward the development of structure by eliminating political parties nominally loyal to him, but organized and controlled by others. In their place he created his own political party, which was unconditionally loyal to him personally. In the 1946 election he had been supported by a small group of dissident Radicals calling themselves the Radical Reorganizing Group and by the hastily organized Labor Party. The latter thought itself the independent voice of the Argentine workers, and as such was anathema to Perón. Very shortly after his inauguration, Perón effected the dissolution of the Radical Reorganizing Group and the Labor Party and replaced them with the Single Party of the Revolution (which, in turn, was reorganized three years later as the Peronist Party). Several of the founders of the Labor Party, notably Luis Gay of the Telephone Workers Union and Cipriano Reyes of the Packinghouse Union, objected strenuously, but they were shunted aside. Most of the government officials, elected under the Labor Party banner, went along with the reorganization. "With the crushing of the *Partido Laborista* in 1946, Perón stamped out the possibility of any incipient political organization of the workers, while at the same time ratifying their union organization—thus reinforcing the fact that the political expression of the working class should pass through him."[35]

In 1947 women were given the right to vote, and shortly after that, Evita formed the Feminine Peronist Party, "so that no Argentine would be denied the privilege of being a Peronist." Women voted for the first time in the presidential election of 1951, and they, even more than men, cast their votes for Juan Perón.[36] Thirty women were elected to Congress that year, all of whom were members of the Feminine Peronist Party.

Evita became extremely popular among the poor. It is not inconceivable that she could have weaned away much of her husband's personal following, but she made no effort to do so. On the contrary, she never tired of repeating that she was honored to be able to serve him. In the preface of her (probably ghost-written) autobiography, which became required reading in all the nation's public schools, she wrote:

> I was not, nor am I, anything more than a humble woman, a sparrow in an immense flock of sparrows, but Perón was, and is, a gigantic condor that flies high and sure among the summits and near to God. If it had not been for him who came down to my level and taught me to fly in another fashion, I would never have known what a condor is like, nor ever have been able to contemplate the marvelous and magnificent immenseness of my people. That is why neither my life nor my heart belongs to me, and nothing of all that I am or have is mine. All that I am, all that I have, all that I think and all that I feel, belongs to Perón.[37]

When Evita died of cancer in mid-1952, her funeral was marked by the greatest outpouring of grief the nation had ever known.[38]

Evita's death deprived Perón of the only follower he fully trusted. Not only was Evita extremely competent, but she was unwaveringly loyal to her husband. Since Perón could not do everything by himself, Evita's death forced him to accelerate the development of structure within the Peronist movement.

Perón's charismatic following was limited largely to the nation's working class. Much of the middle class and virtually all the members of the economic elite opposed him from the very beginning. The large landowners were incensed by many of his early economic policies. For example, even before his inauguration Perón announced the creation of the Argentine Institute for the Promotion of Trade (IAPI), which was given control over the exporting of all major commodities, including the power to fix prices for both producers and consumers. The amount IAPI paid the grain and meat producers was well below the world price for these products, and the profit the government earned was used primarily to support industrialization, especially the newer small industries which had prospered during the war but needed protection in the postwar period. Although perhaps unforeseen by Perón and his economic advisors, the reaction of the large landowners was quite predictable: they simply decreased production. This, plus a decline in the world price for agricultural goods and a series of local droughts, cut export earnings and limited the nation's ability to import.

Perón's rhetoric was intensely antioligarchy, and some of his policies were certainly detrimental to that group, but he stopped short of what the large landowners feared most: the confiscation of their land. As Gary Wynia has written: "What he took from the oligarchy was its government, not its land. It was good populist theater, not revolutionary politics, and ten years later, when Perón fled, the oligarchy was still there, bruised and vengeful, but not seriously damaged by Peronism."[39]

Although Perón did not need the support of the nation's economic elite, he did need the support, or at least the acquiescence, of the military establishment. During the 1946 election campaign the leaders of the armed forces had little choice but to support him; the alternative was a return to the form of civilian administration totally discredited in the eyes of most military leaders. During the early years of his administration Perón's emphasis on industrialization, economic nationalism, and modernization of the armed forces allowed him to retain this support.[40] By 1951, however, an appreciable segment of the military was no longer willing to follow his leadership. During the next four years discontent within the armed forces increased; by 1955 large sectors of the army and almost all the navy had decided that Perón must go.

The first source of friction between Perón and his colleagues in the armed forces was evidently his wife, Evita. As the illegitimate child of a poor provincial family, and later a radio and movie actress, she was not considered fit to be the wife of a high-ranking army officer, much less to be the nation's first lady. Her quasi-revolutionary rhetoric and her openly antimilitary attitude further aggravated the situation. Another source of friction was the anti-clerical position adopted by Perón in 1954 and 1955. Legalization of divorce, abrogation of religious instruction in the public schools, and the jailing or deporting of clergymen caused divided loyalties in Catholic officers.

Most important in the growing anti-Peronism among the leaders of the armed forces was Perón's relationship with the organized labor movement. Never pro-labor, upper middle-class officers were infuriated when the CGT adopted an increasingly arrogant attitude toward the armed forces. Particularly galling was the fact that the CGT managed to have the death penalty reinstated in the Uniform Code of Military Justice. The last straw came in 1955, when Perón appeared to be considering the establishment of armed workers' militias. On September 16, 1955, a military coup forced Perón into an exile from which he did not return for eighteen years.

Anti-Peronist Argentina: The Dispersion of Charisma

Between 1955 and 1958 a provisional administration headed by General Pedro Aramburu attempted to eliminate Peronism from the nation's political landscape. The Peronist Party was outlawed and the leaders of Peronist trade unions were replaced by military men. In subsequent years this anti-Peronism on the part of the leaders of the armed forces became self-perpetuating, as anti-Peronist generals and admirals were responsible for promoting the next generation of officers, and so on. Many officers must have feared that a relaxation of anti-Peronism would leave them open to purges by the Peronists should they return to power. Still, the strongest reason for the anti-Peronism of the leaders of the armed forces was their unwillingness to accept any regime with the power to deprive the military of its role as a political arbiter or to eliminate it as *the* decisive power factor. Between 1955 and 1970 only Peronism, with its massive following among the nation's workers, was a potential threat to the continued hegemony of the armed forces.

In 1958 the armed forces returned power to an elected civilian government. The elections of that year were swept by a faction of the old UCR calling itself the Intransigent Radical Civic Union (UCRI). Its leader, Arturo Frondizi, attained the presidency as a result of a deal with Perón, who traded the votes of his followers for a promise of legality for his party and an end to military intervention in his unions.[41] This bargain gave Frondizi the presidency, but it cost him the ability to govern. Anti-Peronists, civilian as well as military, considered his election tainted and his administration illegitimate.

Frondizi restored legality to Peronism in time for the congressional and gubernatorial elections of 1962. Peronist victories in these elections were the last straw as far as the anti-Peronist military leaders were concerned, however, and Frondizi was deposed. After a year of near total chaos, new elections were held, and once again the Peronists were denied the right to nominate candidates for executive positions. These elections were won by the People's Radical Civic Union (UCRP), the UCR faction that had lost to Frondizi's UCRI five years earlier. The three years of UCRP government were peaceful, but the nation's political problems remained unresolved.

By 1966 the Argentine armed forces had witnessed the failure of two civilian administrations to resolve the "Peronist problem" or to bring about an acceptable rate of economic growth—and these were the administrations of the only two political parties with popular support even approaching that of the Peronists. Still another military coup was the result. The military closed Congress, dissolved all the nation's political parties, and granted near total authority to a retired general, Juan Carlos Onganía.

General Onganía was given four years to fundamentally alter the nature of the nation's social, economic, and political systems; at the end of that period, however, the only change was the advent of widespread political violence. Onganía was deposed, and the army commander-in-chief, General Alejandro Lanusse, assumed the presidency to prepare for another transition to civilian government.

By this time the leaders of the armed forces seem to have realized that for an elected government to be considered legitimate, and thus have any chance to govern effectively, Peronism had to be given complete electoral freedom. Since many military leaders were still opposed to the prospect of a Peronist government, the election law was changed to require a runoff election if no presidential candidate received an absolute majority of the popular vote. (The consensus seemed to be that a Peronist candidate, whoever it might be, might win a plurality of the vote, but would be defeated in a runoff by a coalition of anti-Peronist parties.) Moreover, a series of complicated maneuvers prevented Perón himself from being a candidate.

When the elections were held in March 1973, the Peronist candidate, Héctor Cámpora (whose campaign slogan was "Cámpora to the presidency—Perón to power"), received 49.6 percent of the vote, more than double that of his nearest competitor. General Lanusse decided that the results were close enough to the required absolute majority to cancel the runoff. Only fifty days after his inauguration Cámpora and his vice-president resigned, necessitating new elections in September—this time with Juan Perón as a candidate. Eighteen years and eighteen days after he was forced into exile, Perón was once again inaugurated as president.

When Perón assumed the presidency in 1946 it became difficult for him to maintain frequent, direct communication with his followers. When he was forced into exile it became impossible. Between 1955 and 1973 he appointed—and dismissed—a great many "Personal Delegates," individuals who were supposed to speak, authoritatively, for Perón in Argentina. Seldom were these delegates well known in their own right, and always as soon as they even appeared to be using their own initiative or to be gaining any semblance of popular support, they were summarily dismissed. Perón seemed intent upon making it clear to all that there was no number two person in the movement—that there was only one leader, Juan Domingo Perón.

In urban industrial areas the trade union movement was used as a vehicle of communication between leader and followers. Throughout Perón's exile a near constant stream of Peronist union leaders visited him in Caracas or Santo Domingo or Madrid and brought back tape-recorded messages, which were duplicated and played to the faithful at union meetings.

In the interior, and especially in the more remote provinces, where the union movement was relatively weak, communication was appreciably more difficult. There Perón had no choice but to rely on local politicians who claimed to be unequivocally loyal to him. In those areas where local Peronist leaders gained their own personal following, it was very difficult for Perón to go over their heads and speak directly to the people.

Soon after Perón was forced into exile his movement began to split into two main sections: a syndicalist group, centered in the Federal Capital and its industrial suburbs, and what was commonly referred to as a neo-Peronist group, whose strength was concentrated in the more remote and less developed provinces of the interior. The syndicalist group was by far the larger and the more powerful. Its leaders dominated the CGT—which, with the Peronist Party illegal, served as the organizational base of Peronism at this time—and its vast organizational and financial resources. These new labor leaders, however, were not chosen by Perón. In 1956, when military intervenors were removed from the nation's unions and elections were held to choose new union leaders, those who had held major union positions during Perón's administration were banned as candidates. The post-Perón union leaders were chosen by rank-and-file union members and thus needed to respond to their wishes, which were not necessarily those of Juan Perón.

By 1963 the Peronist unions were themselves divided, further removing Perón from the control he had enjoyed while president. An "orthodox" group of unions, led by José Alonso of the Clothing Workers, was almost unconditionally loyal to Perón, but another group, led by Augusto Vandor of the Metallurgical Workers, appeared to be Peronist in name only. Alonso's group of unions was in vehement opposition to both the Frondizi (1958–1962) and the Illia (1963–1966) administrations. Vandor's group, while claiming to be loyal to Perón, was more likely to negotiate with the government than to confront it; these unions sought at all costs to avoid renewed government intervention in the CGT. The prospect of intervention did not seem to bother Alonso's unions or Perón; in fact, at times they seemed intent upon provoking it.

In spite of this split, the CGT continued to be dominated by Peronist unions. At the time of the 1966 military coup roughly 70 percent of the nation's organized workers belonged to unions led by Peronists. This dominance of the labor movement enabled Peronism to cause major problems for all post-1955 administrations. Typical of the "political" strategies of the Peronist labor movement was its Battle Plan of 1964. The country was divided into eight zones, each of which was subjected to a twenty-four-hour demonstration of labor's ability to seize control of the sources of industrial production. Between May 21 and June 24 more than 11,000 plants were occupied by about 3,200,000 workers.[42]

The neo-Peronism of the interior was essentially a loose alliance of virtually autonomous provincial parties. Lacking strong ties to the CGT, the neo-Peronist parties were almost totally personalistic in nature, and the personality was frequently a local political leader, not Juan Perón. It should not be surprising that neo-Peronism was strongest in the less developed provinces where *caudillismo* continued to play an important role in the political process. In the 1963 elections many of the neo-Peronist parties refused to follow

Perón's order to cast blank ballots[43] to protest the ban on a Peronist presidential candidate. Instead, they nominated their own candidates and obtained sufficient votes to elect two governors, gain control of five provincial legislatures, and win sixteen seats in the lower house of Congress. Of this "disobedience" one neo-Peronist leader later said, "The Neuquén Popular Movement supports the doctrine and the principles of Peronism, but it does not accept its present [local] leadership."[44]

In the congressional elections of 1965, when the Peronists were allowed to nominate their own candidates, many of the local neo-Peronist parties refused to be absorbed into the "official" Peronist party (then called the Popular Union), and thus in some provinces there were two slates of Peronist candidates. Nationally, the Popular Union received about 30 percent of the vote while the various neo-Peronist parties received only 4 percent; however, in every province where there was direct competition between the two it was the neo-Peronists who received the larger number of votes.[45]

In the highly publicized 1965 gubernatorial election in Mendoza there were again two Peronist candidates: a neo-Peronist, representing the local, largely autonomous party, and a Justicialist,[46] representing the nationally organized Peronist party. These two parties split 170,000 votes, allowing victory by the Conservative candidate, who obtained 130,000 votes. In Table 2.2, selected characteristics of Mendoza are correlated with the vote received by

Table 2.2 Rank order correlations between selected county characteristics and the vote for two Peronist gubernatorial candidates, Mendoza, 1965.

Parties	Literacy	Urbani-zation	Agric. Workers	Indus. Workers	Service Workers	White Collar
Official	+.27	+.42	−.47	+.39	+.44	+.24
Neo-Peronist	−.29	−.47	+.73	−.31	−.83	−.43

Source: Darío Canton, *Elecciones y partidos políticos en la Argentina* (Buenos Aires: Siglo Veintiuno Editores, 1973), p. 207.

the two Peronist parties. Unfortunately, all of these variables tap a single underlying dimension: urbanization. Still, the "official" Peronist party fared best in urban counties with large numbers of workers in the secondary and tertiary sectors; neo-Peronism was strongest in counties with large numbers of agricultural workers. Once again, it appeared that those without ties to the trade union movement were the more likely to follow a local *caudillo*.

Within a decade of his overthrow Perón presided over a movement he no longer fully controlled. Many urban workers came to see their national union leader as more relevant to their needs than their former president. And in some of the more remote provinces, the poor, especially the rural poor, looked upon the local Peronist leader as their new *patrón*.

By 1970 there was a far more serious split within Peronism as a result of the formation of what was soon to become the hemisphere's largest and most powerful urban guerrilla group: the Montoneros. There had always been a left-wing faction in Peronism, but until the late 1960s it was virtually insignificant, both in numbers and in influence within the movement. During the 1970s, however, the Montoneros were far from insignificant. Within five years of its birth the organization had five to ten thousand armed members and several times that many supporters and sympathizers.[47]

The original Montoneros, no more than a dozen in number, were uniformly middle-class university students or recent graduates. They were all militant Catholics, many of whom had served as leaders of Catholic lay groups. Although some had earlier been active in extreme right-wing Catholic nationalist groups, by the late 1960s all seemed to have embraced liberation theology or some variant thereof.[48]

Like the Third World Priests, from whom they took their radical Catholicism, the Montoneros were ardent Peronists. However, also like most of the Third World Priests, they were too young to have any direct knowledge of Perón's first administration. They thus tended to have an extremely naive view both of Perón and of

Peronism. Their adoption of Peronism appears to have been based on the assumptions that (1) the Argentine working class was intrinsically revolutionary, (2) Perón was the clear leader of the working class, and therefore (3) Perón was a revolutionary leader.[49]

The Montoneros gained immediate public attention in mid-1970 when they kidnapped and later killed former president Pedro Aramburu. A few weeks later they took over a small town in the province of Córdoba. These and other early actions seem to have been designed to attract public attention, to demonstrate that the Onganía administration was incapable of maintaining law and order, and to gain popular support through daring actions with which the nation's workers might identify.

The immediate goal of the Montoneros was simply to create the conditions under which Perón could return to power. Their bombings, kidnappings, and assassinations were designed to convince the leaders of the armed forces that the only way to restore order was to return to constitutional government. They had no doubt that honest elections would return Perón to the presidency, from which he would lead Argentina to revolutionary socialism.

During the election campaigns of 1973 the Montoneros devoted most of their energies to the mobilization of working-class support for Peronist candidates. Not only did Peronists win the presidential elections (in March with Héctor Cámpora and in September with Perón himself), but they also won large majorities in both houses of Congress and gained control of most provincial governments. Montoneros, running under the Peronist label, won eight seats in the lower house of Congress and close to fifty seats in various provincial legislatures; of even greater utility to them was the election of at least five Montonero sympathizers as provincial governors, including those of the two largest provinces, Buenos Aires and Córdoba.[50]

The Montoneros must have been delighted with the short-lived administration of Héctor Cámpora. Cámpora's first official act was an amnesty decree which released hundreds of Montoneros from prison, including several valued leaders. Cámpora also gave the far left, including the Montoneros as well as other urban guerrilla groups,[51] almost complete control over the national universities, which more than ever became the primary recruiting grounds for guerrillas.

But after only fifty days in office Cámpora and his vice-president resigned, clearing the way for Perón to return to the presidency. Cámpora later claimed that this had been his and Perón's intention from the beginning. This may well have been the case, but it is at least equally possible that Perón, by this time seventy-eight years old and not in good health, would have preferred to make major policy decisions from behind the scene, and to be thought of as the nation's elder statesman who was responsible for a return of peace and prosperity. According to this version of the story, Perón felt compelled to return to the presidency to stop, or even reverse, the drift to the left under Cámpora.

Perón's victory in the September election was a foregone conclusion, but it was important to him and to others that he receive appreciably more votes than had Cámpora six months earlier. The September election gave the Montoneros another opportunity to demonstrate their ability to mobilize working-class support, and this they did. At a Peronist rally on August 31, 150,000 people marched under the Montonero banner.[52] Perón received 62 percent of the vote, the most since 1951, when he also received 62 percent in a race against the same Radical candidate, Ricardo Balbín.

While in exile, Perón had praised the Montoneros, but as soon as he was again inaugurated as president, he made it clear to all—except perhaps to the Montoneros themselves—that Montonero goals as well as methods were anathema to him. At every opportunity, he sided with his movement's labor sector, which was dominated by relatively conservative union bureaucrats. The final break came at the time of Perón's May Day speech in 1974, when he and several Montoneros shouted insults at each other. Perón referred to the Montoneros as "infiltrators who work within and who in terms of treachery are more dangerous than those who work outside." The Montoneros marched away, chanting, "The people are leaving."[53] Although they withdrew their active support of the government, as long as Perón was president the Montoneros did not resume terrorist activities.

A great many Argentines hoped that Perón would work miracles. But on July 1, 1974, less than a year into his third term as president, he died. For thirty years Argentine politics had revolved around the person of Juan Domingo Perón. With his death, the nation began to disintegrate.

★ 3 ★

The Original Following

Impressions of the nature and extent of Juan Perón's charismatic following are found in numerous journalistic accounts and political memoirs of the 1945–1946 period. Although such sources can bring a certain vividness to studies of mass politics, they typically also bring a bias and a narrowness of perspective which make them inadequate as primary data in the study of political behavior. That is precisely the case here. Contempory and retrospective newspaper accounts, as well as reminiscences by key political figures, provide useful—and colorful—information on Peronism emergent, but the data they represent are, to say the very least, limited and unsystematic. They cannot by themselves support an explanation of this charismatic bond.

Yet if it is always true that the student of charisma should not depend on data produced by happenstance sampling and biased observation, it is equally true that what is actually found in the way of systematic evidence for such investigations is almost always less than ideal. The only suitable data base in which a student of Peronist charisma can rigorously investigate the nature of the original following is derived from the 1946 national election returns and the 1947 census. These election and census data, of course, are available only in aggregated form. Moreover, if they are to be employed in a national study, the lowest level at which linkage of the two types of data can occur is that of the county.[1]

Whatever the level of aggregation, such "ecological" data present numerous problems of analysis and interpretation. We will discuss these difficulties below. First, however, we give detailed attention to the earlier data-based studies which have sought unsuccessfully to specify the original nature of Peronism. This detail, perhaps more than is customary, is provided here to underscore one point: that the particulars of methodology are crucial to the validity of research conclusions.

Previous Research

Although the Argentine presidential election of 1946 may have inspired more commentary than any other ever held in Latin America, there have been only three systematic studies of it.[2] Each of these studies employed ecological analysis, by which is meant statistical analysis of aggregate voting and census data. The first, published in 1972, was "The Social Base of Peronism," by Peter Smith.[3] This was followed the next year by Gino Germani's study, "El surgimiento del Peronismo: El rol de los obreros y de los migrantes internos"[4]—which provoked a reply by Smith: "Las elecciones argentinas de 1946 y las inferencias ecológicas."[5] And the year after that E. Spencer Wellhofer published "The Mobilization of the Periphery: Perón's 1946 Triumph."[6]

Questions about the nature and extent of Perón's original support were addressed, but not answered, by these studies. A fundamental reason for these unanswered questions is the failure of the investigators to cope with the cross-level inference problems presented by ecological data. Each study sought to draw conclusions about individuals but lacked the data and/or the methods which might have made this a reasonable prospect.

Inference problems aside, the conclusions in these studies are far from consensual. Smith argued that in what he called the big cities—in actuality, counties which contained big cities—"the 'old' laboring groups played a more crucial role than did internal migrants," while in "townships"—counties which contained towns of 2,000 to 50,000 people—"Perón attracted votes from both urban and rural lower-class groups."[7] Germani insisted that migrants were more important in Perón's victory than were organized workers; in fact, a large part of his 1973 article is an attack of Smith's contrary conclusion.[8] And Wellhofer concluded that "early Peronist support appears as an admixture of recently migrated lower strata in the city of Buenos Aires and its suburbs, the previously registered but apathetic voters in the province of Buenos Aires and the previously mobilized but peripheral lower strata in the interior."[9]

Even ignoring cross-level inference problems, one cannot reconcile these claims by returning to the original studies. Other conceptual and methodological flaws undermine their conclusions. For example, both Smith and Wellhofer take crucial independent variables—the occupational data—from the published version of the 1947 census, which reports this occupational data by place of employment rather than place of residence (where one votes). The occupational data for many geographic units is thus distorted in unknown, but surely important, ways. A very large, but unascertainable, number of people in the Federal Capital live, and thus vote, in a census unit other than the one in which they work. In greater Mendoza (which straddles three different counties) and in the Buenos Aires suburbs the same is true.

A problem of equal seriousness lies in the operationalization of key variables. Smith, for example, measures industrial white-collar employment as "the average number of employees [*empleados*] per industry" and industrial blue-collar employment as "the percentage of industrial employees who are workers [*obreros*]."[10] Under this scheme, a county with one industrial plant employing five people, all of whom are blue-collar workers, has an industrial blue-collar score of 100, while another county of the same population with ten plants and 1,000 employees, 600 of whom are blue-collar workers, receives a score of 60. Commercial white- and blue-collar employment figures are derived in the same manner. Using these measures, Smith finds, not surprisingly, that across all of Argentina's 365 counties occupation is virtually uncorrelated with Perón's vote percentage.[11]

Wellhofer, working primarily at the level of provinces rather than counties, unaccountably uses the percentage of turnout in 1946 as his indicator of turnout *surge* among previous nonvoters. Thus Tucumán, where turnout in 1946 was 79 percent, is assumed to have had more previous nonvoters than Salta, where turnout was 72 percent. Yet this is demonstrably false. Previous nonvoting was 25 percent in Tucumán and 45 percent in Salta.[12] Wellhofer also uses the percentage of change in registration from 1940 to 1946 as an indicator of internal migration. In every province this is a positive figure. Obviously more than migration is involved here, but were the only other factor ordinary population growth, the indicator might still be of use. Such, unfortunately, is not the case. Because of highly differential patterns of settlement by earlier immigrants (who almost all remained outside the electorate), there is in some provinces very substantial growth as a result of entry by the second generation into the electorate. This factor, especially important to the growth of the 1940s electorates in large cities and their suburbs, undermines the usefulness of Wellhofer's indicator. Finally, Wellhofer uses the percentage of the vote received by the Socialist Party in 1942 as his indicator of numbers in the "lower strata." By this measure, those strata collectively range only from 1 percent in Mendoza to 5 percent in Tucumán. Even as a correlate of class this is a dubious measure. The evidence available indicates that the Socialist Party had very limited and highly specialized appeal among Argentine workers of that day. Hence its vote cannot be taken as a proxy for numbers of workers or even for numbers of activist workers present in the population of a province or county.[13]

Germani's confusions (again, aside from the problems inherent in cross-level inference) are of a different, primarily statistical, character. One involves his insistence that occupational categories should be calculated as a percentage of the economically active population rather than of total population, because "in the case of electoral analysis what one is interested in is the demographic and social composition of the electorate rather than the total active population."[14] It is to his credit that Germani even considered alternative denominators for his ratio variables; the other investigators apparently felt that the choice of denominator made no difference, a mistake we consider below. However, the rationale for

Germani's choice is shaky. It is true that the economically active population more closely resembles the electorate than does total population, but the resemblance is far from perfect. In 1946 the electorate was composed of male citizens above the age of seventeen; the economically active population included foreign born (who comprised 15 percent of the population), women (about 10 percent of whom were engaged in industry, business or services), and persons between the ages of fourteen and seventeen. These "distortions" cannot be assumed to have been evenly or randomly distributed across electoral units. Indeed, the opposite is true. Germani himself earlier pointed out that 41 percent of the adult males in the Federal Capital were foreign born, and that very few of them had become naturalized citizens.[15]

Most damaging to Germani's analysis is the level of collinearity between his independent variables. The major point of substantive disagreement between Smith and Germani deals with the relative importance of migrants and urban workers in determining the Perón vote. These two (percentaged) variables are correlated at .99 in Germani's data. In the set of counties he analyzed, those places which had large numbers of migrants also had large numbers of workers *because most of the migrants were workers*. Germani was well aware of this fact—he emphasized that within greater Buenos Aires 73 percent of the members of the working class were migrants.[16] Yet he did not seem to understand the implications of this for his statistical analysis and consequently produced coefficients of a dubious character (for example, standardized regression coefficients well above unity).

Smith recognized that multicollinearity was at least potentially a problem. In his reply to Germani, he commented that "an important problem that Germani does not mention is the possible existence of multicollinearity."[17] But this recognition did not lead him to pertinent questions about either Germani's findings or his own. It is true that in his earlier piece, Smith had offered a reassurance, in a footnote to an appendix, that in his data the maximum correlation between any pair of independent variables was .56.[18] However, this reassurance ignored the possibility of multicollinearity.

Other statistical foibles in this literature include Germani's use of a method, stepwise regression, which is both capricious and atheoretical, in his effort to build explanatory models,[19] and Wellhofer's unnecessary sampling of aggregate observations, reducing an N of 118 to 25 in order "to reduce calculations."[20]

Finally, none of these studies makes a serious attempt to explain the 1946 Perón vote across the nation as a whole. Wellhofer examines six provinces, one at a time; Smith divides his analysis into three parts, looking at counties which contain large cities, those which include smaller towns, and those which have no urban area; Germani runs separate analyses according to the size of a county's largest urban area but ignores those counties which have no town of 5,000 or more people—about 70 percent of the total. Each author comes up with a somewhat different explanation for the Perón vote for each geographic arena, but none of them offers any theoretical rationale for these differences.

It should be emphasized that these three authors published their work nearly fifteen years ago, at a time when a great many social scientists were feeling their way through the world of methodology and statistics. Their errors were not particularly unusual for that period. It is more surprising to see the absence of theory either preceding or deriving from these three empirical forays. In any case there can be no doubt that this body of work fails to provide us with definition or understanding of the initial mass response to Perón.

Aggregate Data Problems

Aggregate data—that is, data describing collections of people (usually geographically based) rather than individuals—have long been an indispensable source of evidence in political analysis.[21] Until the 1940s there was little else available for systematic studies of mass behavior. Reliable observations at the individual level were almost nonexistent. However, data describing the voting behavior of neighborhoods, townships, counties, or provinces were readily obtainable and often could be merged with data describing the social ecologies and economic circumstances of those units. Moreover, such observations sometimes were available in time-series form, providing the opportunity for dynamic studies with historical sweep.

The development of survey research methods during and after World War II shifted the attention of most students of political behavior to microdata, collected from probability samples of relevant populations by means of direct interviews. This wholesale shift did not occur because aggregate data are inherently deficient and individual level data inherently superior. Well-known and difficult problems with interview data include a variety of "presentation of self" biases,[22] response sets,[23] and even self-delusions;[24] "attitudes" can turn out to be chimerical;[25] measurement contamination by interviewers and coders can be difficult to control. The great attraction of microdata is that they are collected at the level where theoretical interest very often is focused. Obviously, the data most suitable for any study depend on the question being asked. If one is concerned with a theory about aggregates—for example, about groups, electorates, or entire cultures—then collective properties will be in point. If one is explaining the behavior of decision makers, voters, or adherents to a cause, then individual level data are much to be preferred.

Yet it remains nearly as true today as in the past that for many theoretically fascinating *micro*analytic questions in the social sciences, there are no suitable *micro*data available. This is especially true when the questions have historical dimension. The techniques and the limits of aggregate data analysis thus remain focal concerns for many students of political behavior.

In the present chapter we focus on voting in the 1946 election. (But note that voting is here a proxy for what we are really interested in: devotion to Juan Perón. There is a problem with this proxy measure, which we will come back to.) As we noted at the outset, the only data available for this investigation describe aggregates—electoral precincts in the Federal Capital and counties for the remainder of the country. Though we would like to know what sorts of *people* voted for Perón, the answers coming most clearly from our data will tell us what sorts of *places* generated more or less support for him. In other words, we will present evidence which ties the 1946 Perón electoral victory to certain ecological settings. The question, of course, will be why *these* settings?

By now it is well known that drawing conclusions about the behavior of individuals from findings about the populations of geographically based aggregates—for example, precincts, wards, communities, or provinces—is tricky, to say the least. To appreciate that point, one need only consider the old example in which an observer discovers that places where many physicians work are very likely to be places where many people are ill. This strong correlation probably does not mean that the doctors are making people ill; nor is it likely to mean that doctors themselves are ill. By the same token, in political research a strong correlation between incidence of industrial employment and incidence of Peronist voting does not necessarily mean that workers voted for Perón. Such a conclusion would fall victim to the "ecological fallacy." In simplest terms, that fallacy—and its opposite, the "individualistic fallacy" (in which individual-level data are used for conclusions about the properties of collectivities)—involves the incorrect belief that a correlation found at one level of analysis is also to be found at a higher or lower level of analysis.

The conditions under which cross-level inference does or does not make sense have been the subject of a large body of statistical work over the last twenty years.[26] The technique most often employed in these investigations is ecological regression—multiple regression using ecological (for example, aggregate voting and census) data. Properly handled, it is a powerful means of assigning causal weights to the various contextual factors believed to be important to, say, a particular electoral outcome. But when we seek to make inferences about those weights at the individual level, Donald Stokes has aptly described the undertaking as "a game against nature."[27] Nature is holding the cards, and the investigator is trying to peek. In the spirit of that metaphor, he writes: "Investigators who resort to these techniques are typically allowed to see data only in aggregated form, from which they must discern relationships at some other level of analysis often having to do with the behavior of individual persons. The investigator who plays this game well will have the most sensitive regard for the stratagems which his 'adversary' may have used in aggregating the data that are revealed from those that remain hidden. Early investigators might have avoided serious mistakes if they had tried to say what stratagems would have made their analysis techniques plausible."[28]

The complex schemes which can lie behind the cards are not easily deciphered. Essentially, one is trying to figure out why the data fall the way they do—a routine part of any data analysis. The special problem lies in the fact that inside the observed collectivities there exist complex social worlds in which many, many factors— some obvious and others not—may be interrelated. When one taps into these networks by measuring one or another property, the trick is to determine what has been measured—merely the obvious and intended target, or a set of subtle and unexpected correlates of that target. What, in other words, does the empirical indicator really get at? Because of such complexities, we see in some ecological analyses the type of finding where an independent variable which ranges, say, from 1 to 5 percent will "explain" a dependent variable which ranges from 40 to 90 percent. Or we might find a study in which raw numbers "show" that the presence of each additional worker in a district predicts fourteen additional votes for a labor candidate.

The confusion inherent in such an exercise is compounded when the aggregate units involved are of great size and thus likely to have within them numerous and complex social networks. But it is no solution to focus attention on a *few* small units. A reduction in network complexity may well be purchased at the price of a great increase in idiosyncrasy. The social and economic peculiarities that were averaged out in the larger units emerge as central to the behavior of the smaller ones. The ideal circumstance for the eco-logical analyst is that where a *large number* of *small units* are the objects of the analysis. However, this rarely occurs.

The conclusion to be drawn from the last two decades of meth-odological work on cross-level inference is that even in the best of circumstances the researcher using aggregate data is highly constrained. It may be possible to estimate the marginal effects of particular types of individuals—that is, the effect when all other causally relevant factors have been held constant—but it will not be possible to estimate gross effects.[29] In the present research we may be able to determine the contributions, *all else equal*, of various types of individuals to Perón's victory, but we will not be able to deal with the question of how particular social groups allocated their votes.

It is often the case that units in an ecological study are of vastly different size. For example, in Wellhofer's analysis of Peronist voting, the data describe provinces which at that time ranged in population from 4,300,000 to 110,000. Such differentials generally lead to the use of ratio variables—that is, variables in which the original measures are divided by population size—because the original measures all yield values which are in very large part a function of a common base. Without somehow controlling for size, multicollinearity among independent variables may undermine any attempt to assess effects. Moreover, the relationship between dependent and independent variables may be close, possibly very close, due solely to the common size factor.

Per capita numbers, however, bring their own problems. In shifting attention away from raw numbers, percentages direct our gaze to relative scores. For example, in a voting study the dependent variable no longer measures how well a candidate did in each district but how well the candidate did, given the district's population size. The variance in the second is likely to be unrelated to the variance in the first. And for some analysts, especially political practitioners, explaining the variance in the second may well be of little interest.

The percentage measure also can be troublesome when the geographic districts of a country are split into a few which have most of the population and many others which have very little—a capital city versus countryside dichotomy. In the extreme version of this situation, virtually all of the political action is in the capital city. Yet once absolute numbers are converted to per capita figures, the crucial arena of the capital city loses its distinctiveness and visibility, becoming merely one of many. The variance in these districts' relative scores may be unrelated to anything which is very important about the election and which may, in fact, be so idiosyncratic as to be beyond the reach of any statistical explanation.

Investigators using ratio variables rarely offer any rationale for their choices of denominators. And yet these choices are certainly no trivial matter. We have found, for example, that the correlation between the percentage of industrial workers and the percentage of the vote for Perón ranges between -0.155 and $+0.420$, depending upon the denominator employed. In addition, as will be seen in what follows, the choice of denominators is not perfectly straightforward.

Analysis of ratios can compound the problems of aggregate data in more technical ways as well. In the mid-1970s Eric Uslaner, William Vanderbok, and Adam Przeworski and Fernando Cortes all cautioned against the indiscriminate use of ratio variables (echoing a warning issued by Karl Pearson some eighty years earlier).[30] Pearson's point was that ratios with a common denominator (X/Z and Y/Z) may be correlated even thought their components (X, Y, and Z) are not. From this came the more general point that the use of ratio variables can lead to biased estimates in ordinary least squares (OLS) regression. This argument recently has been rejected by Firebaugh,[31] who contends that the spurious relationship between ratios is a problem of correlation analysis, but not regression analysis. In what seems to us a restatement of Przeworski and Cortes, Firebaugh points out that in regression analysis the y intercept acts as a diagnostic tool: if it is not zero, that indicates that the ratios are correlated even though their components are not. However, Firebaugh goes beyond this to state that "ratios cause no problems in regression analysis."[32] This claim seems to be based on the fact that in aggregate data analysis it often is necessary to used weighted least squares (WLS) to deal with inconstant error variance. It is true that WLS creates ratios, but it does so in a way rather different from that used in most analyses with per capita data. Moreover, even with per capitized data, WLS quite often is needed—thus creating ratios of ratios.

We do not find much useful guidance in Firebaugh's work, nor, for that matter, in the writings of the others. Uslaner ultimately advises only that researchers be guided by theory. Vanderbok suggests the use of residuals (from regressions of all variables on population)—an approach which, as Lyons[33] points out, would produce biased estimates in the model. In the end, it seems that choices will be forced upon the analyst by the nature of the data. When observations on both dependent and independent variables are overwhelmingly a function of population size, multicollinearity will force the use of ratios. When observations are not overwhelmingly a function of population size, the simple variables are to be preferred. We will return to the matter of numbers versus ratios in our analysis of county-level data below.

Data and Indices

The dependent variable in this analysis is the Perón vote in the 1946 election. This variable serves as a proxy for what we are really interested in, commitment to Juan Perón. A charismatic bond involves much more than mere support for a leader. Its most distinctive characteristic is its passion. A national election, especially a highly charged one such as Argentina's in 1946, provides observable arenas in which charismatic followers may act out—in street demonstrations, in campaign mobilizations, and finally in voting itself —their feeling for their leader-candidate. But when the final vote is tallied, the total will not come solely from those true believers. Mixed in will be votes which have come from citizens who were no more than mildly impressed or perhaps who simply preferred Perón to a less attractive alternative.

When a charismatic following is a very small fraction of the total supporting vote in an election, its numbers and location are likely to be hidden. This is true, of course, not just at the national level but also at the lower levels typically used in ecological studies. But if the fraction represented by the charismatic following is very large, analysis of the following by substituting aggregate voting totals is reasonable. A question of immediate importance, then, is the size of the bloc of fervent Peronists in 1946.

Let us begin with our conclusion: it is clear that Perón's 1946 victory was not due entirely to his passionate followers, but it seems to us equally clear that their weight in that victory was very great. Perón's total vote was just under 1.5 million. The overwhelming majority of these votes were not "delivered" by some organization having deep roots and long standing in Argentine political life.[34] Instead, the votes were truly volunteered for a new figure on the political stage. We can begin to estimate the share of the total vote which came from Perón's most passionate devotees by examining the size of the demonstrations for him on October 17, 1945. Some observers claimed that participants in the main demonstration in the Federal Capital numbered half a million,[35] but a more conservative figure (on which there is broader agreement) is 300,000.[36] Added to that number must be tens of thousands more who attended lesser demonstrations occurring in provincial urban centers about the same time.[37] Factored in, too, must be an unknown but surely vast number of Peronists who did not attend demonstrations, no doubt for the most mundane of reasons—they were unaware of them, had conflicting obligations, lived or worked too far from the action, and so on. Putting all of this together, we find it not unrealistic to assume a total charismatic following exceeding 500,000. Subtracting a generous figure to allow for nonvoting participants (primarily women and those who were underage), we end up with what we believe to be a conservative estimate: at least one out of four Perón votes in 1946 came from his true believers.

This fraction is large enough to be reassuring on the point of sheer numbers; the charismatic following was not swamped by a mass of lukewarm Peronist voters. We are less sanguine on the question of the constancy of the fraction across all of the districts in the analysis. The true-believer share of the Peronist vote probably was higher in the industrial suburbs ringing the major cities and lower elsewhere. Recall that theory predicts (and, as noted in Chapter 2, journalistic evidence suggests) that a special response to Perón's magic was to be found among the "seekers" who had flooded into the cities from a depressed rural economy. We assume that it would be in such places—where Perón's wage policies were most keenly felt and his street camaraderie most visible—that the ratio of true believers to total supporters would be higher. No adjustment to the vote figures is dictated by this assumption. However, the analysis to follow must be read with awareness of the imperfection of the dependent variable as an estimate of Perón's charismatic following.

This chapter relies primarily on two sets of data for its analyses. The smaller of the two describes the 209 *circuitos* (precincts) of the Federal Capital (the city of Buenos Aires). For each precinct, the results from the 1946 election have been combined with data which describe the precinct's socioeconomic makeup. Note, however, that these data on socioeconomic status are from 1959, not 1946. They were obtained by sampling the registration forms for all male registrants in that year. From this sample (10 percent of the total), occupation and literacy information for each registrant was obtained. The usefulness of these data for describing 1946 conditions depends on the social and economic stability of the 209 precincts between 1946 and 1959. The original collector of these data tested that stability using a subsample drawn from 1945 registration forms and reports "no significant changes" in those fourteen years.[38] Stability statistics are lacking; however, relying upon his overall characterization, we will use these data to study the social ecology of Perón's support in the Federal Capital.

The main data set describes the entire country in terms of 1946 election results and 1947 census findings. Thus it includes all of the pertinent data used by Smith and Germani. The lowest level at which these national election and census data can be merged is that of the county, or in the Federal Capital, the ward.

Our census data differ from that of Smith (but not Germani) in one crucial respect: the occupational data—hand copied from the unpublished Table 41 of the 1947 National Census—are aggregated by place of residence, and hence place of voting, rather than place of employment. Also important to note is the fact that our national data set was purged—through a variety of consistency checks—of numerous errors in the original file.

Finally, a word should be said about "missing data" problems.

The economic and social change sweeping across Argentina in the decade preceding Juan Perón's triumphant election make time-series observations especially important for this study, yet such data do not exist. No census was taken during the period. Indeed, no census was taken in the four decades preceding 1947. Some national economic data are available from other sources, but this level of aggregation undermines much of the usefulness of the data. Election data for the period between 1930 and 1946 period are available at the level of the province but not, for the most part, below that level. Therefore we cannot follow changes in the size and behavior of the Argentine electorate at the level at which the investigation would be most worthwhile. The time-series analyses potentially most useful are beyond our reach.

Turnout: National and Provincial Results

Our point of departure in examining the initial mass response to Juan Perón is to examine voter turnout in the 1946 election. In absolute numbers, that turnout reached 2.8 million, a jump of 800,000 over the vote in the previous presidential election in 1937 and a near doubling of the extraordinary 1928 vote, when Yrigoyen ran for his second presidential term.

More interesting than the absolute turnout numbers—which partially reflect in their increases the natural (but dramatic) growth of the electorate from 1928 to 1946—are their relative counterparts. For many years election analysts have known that the ebb and flow of voters as a fraction of registrants can be an important indicator of the mood of an electorate. Angus Campbell,[39] for example, showed the strong link between a surge in turnout and increased intensity of political feeling. W. D. Burnham[40] found such electoral mobilization to be an important hallmark of realignment in the politics of a nation. In light of this and related work, we would be surprised to see the emergence of a charismatic candidate *not* accompanied by a jump in relative electoral involvement, possibly fed by those in fervent opposition as well as those in fervent support. (Of course, one must be careful here; a surge in mass turnout does not *establish* the presence of a charismatic bond.)

The 1946 national turnout meets these expectations but not unambiguously. It was the highest turnout level ever seen in Argentina, 83.3 percent, surpassing the 80.8 percent in the still unexplained Yrigoyen surge of 1928 and also topping the 76.1 percent in the preceding (1937) presidential contest. Still, the 1946 turnout plainly is not an enormous national surge. Two factors make it more impressive. The first is that it occurred in a system where nonvoting was punishable by a fine and/or civil penalties.[41] Previous research has shown that even small fines elevate turnout substantially, in the process reducing the visibility of any conversion to "voluntary" electoral behavior.[42] In the present case this means that the aggregated mass response to Perón had two components: a visible one involving the turnout surge noted above and an invisible one involving the conversion of previous voters from electoral behavior which is obligatory and pro forma to that which is voluntary and committed. This latter group we cannot measure, but in light of Perón's victory it certainly must have been much larger than the former. Nonetheless, the size of the surge group is striking in light of immediately preceding election turnout figures (and possibly also in light of the "ceiling effect," which makes increases progressively harder to achieve when population proportions are moving to very high levels).

The second factor making the observable surge impressive is that it occurred in an electorate flooded in the preceding decade by the sorts of people classically found to be politically disengaged: recent migrants—usually of very limited education and often registered in their distant places of origin rather than in current place of residence—and the offspring of families of European origin who had remained deliberately apolitical, in most cases failing even to acquire Argentine citizenship. With an electorate including hundreds of thousands of such people, the challenge—even in a setting of compulsory voting—is to keep turnout levels from falling. That the levels should have grown substantially in 1946 must be judged in this context.

Further insight into the effect of Perón's candidacy on the turnout of 1946 can be gained by examining the behavior over time of the two areas where half the Argentine population resided: the Federal Capital and the province of Buenos Aires. Figure 3.1 presents the turnout pattern for each of these areas and for the nation as a whole.

Examine first the pattern for the nation. The decline from the turnout surge of 1928 is visible in the early 1930s, but is reversed in the elections of 1936 and 1937 (the latter a presidential contest), and then falls off again until Perón's election in 1946. More revealing of the nature of the Perón surge are the turnout tracks for the Federal Capital and Buenos Aires province. The former, for more than a hundred years the center of Argentine political life, shows from 1928 a rather steady decline in turnout, relieved only by a small increase in 1937 and, to a lesser extent, in 1946. Looking only at presidential contests, we find that in 1928 the turnout was

Figure 3.1 Voter turnout, 1928–1946. Source: Darío Canton, *Materiales para el estudio de la sociología política en la Argentina,* vol. 1 (Buenos Aires: Editorial del Instituto [Torcuato DiTella], 1968), pp. 101–129.

92 percent, in 1937, 88 percent, and in 1946, when turnout in the rest of the nation was surging, only 83 percent. The Federal Capital's fall and the rest of the nation's surge brought their turnout figures together in 1946 for the first time in modern Argentine history.

Not surprisingly, Buenos Aires province, which held the industrial suburbs and *villas miserias* ringing the capital city, in 1946 behaved very differently from the Federal Capital. Its turnout surge that year was, by any standard, dramatic. For the first time ever voters in the province of Buenos Aires turned out in the same proportion as those in the Federal Capital.

Returning to the entire set of provinces, we find that variance in 1946 turnout was quite small—half that seen in any previous presidential election. The Perón surge was relatively invariant, as well. Both figures point up the evenness of the Peronist effect on turnout at the provincial level.

Perón won the election of 1946 with 52.4 percent of the national vote. His support across the provinces ranged from a high of 71 percent in Tucumán to a low of 34 percent in San Juan. Contrary to what might have been expected from the comparison of turnout in the Federal Capital and Buenos Aires province, these two areas were not very different in their support for Perón, giving him 53.0 percent and 54.8 percent, respectively.

Turnout: County-Level Analysis

Statistical analysis of turnout in the 365 counties must begin by confronting the problem of skewed distributions. In the data set there are a small number of counties with large populations and a large number of counties with small populations. This means that on every population-based variable—for example, registrants, voters, Peronists, workers, youth, and migrants—the distribution is badly skewed, with many counties bunching up at one end and a few counties pulling the tail of the distribution way out at the other.

As noted above, one way to cope with this is to turn the raw numbers into per capita percentages. Such a solution, however, seems straightforward but very often is not. One frequently troubling question is which denominator to use. Consider the present case, which is not unusual. We are using census and electoral data. The dependent variable for an analysis of turnout would most often be voters divided by registrants. The independent variables, however, would have as numerators urban population, illiterate population, industrial workers, and so on. Registrants, the dependent variable denominator, is a group almost entirely made up of Argentine-born males, eighteen and over. However, "industrial workers" includes males *and* females (though no doubt overwhelmingly male, here), native *and* foreign born, and those between fourteen and eighteen years old as well as those eighteen and over. Similar problems exist with the other measures. The only available census denominators in the data set are population, Argentine males, all males, and males fourteen and over. Between the census denominators and the electoral denominators there is no good fit. Of course, one could use different denominators for the census variables and the electoral variables. But whatever the choices, we know that in substantive terms the denominators used make a real difference. Findings and interpretations of findings hang on this decision.

Another way to cope with the skewness in the variables' distributions is to normalize the data by using a suitable transformation, in this case the base 10 logarithm of each variable. A conclusive argument against this method could be made if the resulting numbers were perfectly or nearly perfectly colinear, in pairs or in combinations, simply as a function of population size. That is not true here. Hence, avoiding the denominator problem, we use logged variables in conducting our county-level turnout analysis. Another advantage to this approach is a more straightforward interpretation of the coefficients generated by the technique we rely upon, regression analysis.[43]

In the county-level analysis of voting turnout we begin with the simplest possible model, in which vote (V_L^*) is predicted by registration (R_L). Here are the estimates for such an equation:

$$(3.1) \qquad V_L^* = -0.22 + 1.03R_L$$
$$(-15.2) \quad (293.5)$$

$$R^2 = .994 \qquad N = 364$$

Here V_L^* = the estimated number of votes (logged) and R_L = the logged number of registrants; the figures in parentheses are corrected (WLS) t-ratios; R^2 = the estimated coefficient of determination; N = the number of observations.[44]

There is, of course, no surprise in the goodness of fit statistic for this model. Virtually all of the variance in the vote is statistically "explained" by registration, which is only to state the obvious: voting and registration numbers both reflect population size. However, note the model's slope coefficient ($b = 1.03$). In interpreting that coefficient, understand that with both the independent and dependent variables logged, as here, one is dealing with *proportionate* change; the slope coefficient gives the percent change in the dependent variable for every percent change in the independent variable.[45] Thus, in Equation 3.1 we see that V_L^* changes 1.03 percent of its range when R_L changes only 1 percent of its range. This means that R_L has a slight accelerating impact on V_L^*, or in ordinary language, that in 1946 larger counties—that is, counties with more registrants—had a somewhat greater vote "yield" than did smaller counties.

Further insight into the turnout for this election can be gained by examining the error in this model. Even though the model predicts higher turnout levels in more populous counties, the residuals for Buenos Aires province show its turnout level to have been higher still: the median county level was 0.42 standard deviations above expectation and the total vote for the province exceeded the model's prediction by nearly 24,000. Even more interesting, almost half of that vote excess came from the large counties adjacent to the Federal Capital—that is, the working-class suburbs of the capital city—which had a median turnout 1.07 standard deviations above expectation. Indeed, of the eleven counties farthest above expectation in absolute terms, four were from the suburbs of the Federal Capital. These results reinforce both the mobilization theory advanced in Chapter 1 and the time-series findings reported above. Also in keeping with the latter is the finding here that the wards of the Federal Capital did not significantly depart, in either relative or absolute terms, from the expectations established by the overall turnout model.

The other notable departures from expected turnout level in absolute terms were found for the industrial provinces of Córdoba (about 10,000 more votes cast than the model predicted) and Santa Fe (about 11,000 more). Rosario, the great industrial county of the latter province, was the unit having the single greatest "excess" vote, 2,800 above the expected value. At the low end, both Santiago del Estero and Tucumán had turnouts 11,000 lower than predicted by the model. Inexplicably, the unit falling farthest below the expectation was the capital city of Tucumán, where the vote was 6,000 lower than expected.

Taken together, these findings on turnout are in keeping with— but obviously not final proof of—the contention that political passions were strong in the context of the 1946 election *and* that such passions were concentrated in those sectors of Argentine society which we have argued were responsive to Perón as a charismatic leader. In retrospect, probably all students of Argentine politics would agree that 1946 was a critical election, representing a fundamental realignment of that nation's political forces, a realignment continuing to this very day. But whether that realignment can be tied more definitively to charismatic bonding depends on the analysis of Perón's own vote.

Support for Perón: National Analyses

Perón won the 1946 election with 1,490,000 votes, 52.4 percent of the total. His margin of victory was nearly 10 percent. The Federal Capital and two of the three large provinces—Buenos Aires and Santa Fe—gave Perón similar support levels, 53, 55, and 55 percent, respectively. The remaining large province, Córdoba, was markedly different, giving him only 42 percent. Among the small provinces, Tucumán stands out for the extraordinary strength of its response to Perón (71 percent) and San Juan for the opposite (34 percent).

Our preliminary analysis of these results involves two basic regression models, with all variables logged to normalize distributions. The first model is the obvious one: Perón's vote (P_L^*) is described as a simple function of the total number of voters (V_L). Here are the estimates for such a "vote share" model:

$$(3.2) \quad P_L^* = -0.66 + 1.09V_L$$
$$(-12.5) \quad (82.9)$$
$$R^2 = .912 \quad N = 364$$

where P_L^* = the estimated Perón vote (logged); V_L = the total number of votes (logged); and the statistics as in Equation 3.1.

The coefficient of determination shows that the model describes the data quite well, no surprise in light of the population factor involved on both sides of the equation. The interesting feature of the model is its slope coefficient. Again we see an acceleration function, and this time it is more pronounced. Perón's vote share gets progressively higher as we move from smaller to larger populations. Both industrial workers and recent migrants, of course, were to be found in the populous urban locales.

Important questions to address with this model are where the Perón vote was appreciably above that expected by the model, and where appreciably below. This may be examined in either absolute or relative terms. In taking the absolute view, one asks how many *votes* above or below expectation did a unit deliver. In taking the relative view, one asks what is a unit's standardized distance from the regression line, with no reference to the unit's population size. Provincial-level answers to both questions are found in Table 3.1.

In absolute terms two locations are dramatic in their above-expectation vote for Perón, the suburbs of the Federal Capital with an excess of 24,500 and the province of Tucumán with an excess of 25,100. Also notable is the remainder of Buenos Aires province with an excess of 14,800. The below-expectation vote is remarkable in Córdoba, a perennial stronghold of the Radical Party, where

Table 3.1   The Perón vote, 1946: Deviations from the vote predicted by Equation 3.2.

District	Absolute[a]	Relative[b]
Federal Capital	−10.0	−0.25
Capital suburbs	+24.5	+0.86
Buenos Aires	+14.8	+0.18
Catamarca	+3.2	+0.53
Córdoba	−30.8	−1.15
Corrientes	−9.0	−1.09
Entre Ríos	−3.8	−0.06
Jujuy	+5.6	+0.91
La Rioja	+2.2	+0.67
Mendoza	+4.2	+0.54
Salta	+8.0	+0.65
San Juan	−6.7	+0.55
San Luis	−0.0	−0.12
Santa Fe	+5.5	+0.41
Santiago del Estero	+5.4	+0.32
Tucumán	+25.1	+1.51

a. In thousands of votes.
b. Median county difference in standard deviations.

Perón's vote was 30,800 under that predicted, and in the Federal Capital, where it was 10,000 low.

The relative numbers give a somewhat different picture. (The median is used here, instead of the mean, to avoid distortions due to anomalous distributions.) Among the large provinces, the Federal Capital, Santa Fe, and the bulk of Buenos Aires (that is, with the suburbs of the Federal Capital excluded) are reasonably well predicted by the model. Only Córdoba stands apart, showing in these relative terms the same kind of below par Perón vote (median county deficiency = −1.15 standard deviations) which appears in the absolute numbers. The Radicals in this province had not only great but also widely distributed strength. The suburbs of the Federal Capital on average give support 0.86 standard deviations above expectation. Among the politically less important provinces, Tucumán is especially supportive and Corrientes especially unsupportive.

At their extremes, the absolute departures from expectations also can usefully be examined at the county level. The most notable cases in terms of Perón deficiency are for the most part found in Córdoba (three out of the bottom four counties) plus La Plata, the capital of Buenos Aires province, and Pilar, an upper-class ward in the Federal Capital. At the upper end the great Perón surpluses come from three locations: the suburbs of the Federal Capital, an exemplar being Avellaneda; the counties of Tucumán; and, most of all, the industrial county of Rosario.

The second preliminary model with which we examine the Perón vote takes registration, instead of total vote, as its concern. It differs from the previous model in the obvious fact that registration includes both voters *and* nonvoters. Thus, the question addressed here is how well—or how poorly—Perón fared relative to expectations, when expectations are established by the overall registration figures. The importance of this question is made clear when one recognizes that turnout significantly influences the meaning of "doing well" in an election. In any electoral district, one may simultaneously do well in vote share and do poorly in registration share, if turnout is small. Moreover, our primary concern with mobilization of supporters by a charismatic leader is better addressed when nonparticipation is not ignored, as in the vote-share models.

$$(3.3) \quad P_L^* = -0.91 + 1.22 R_L$$
$$(16.3) \quad (89.2)$$
$$R^2 = .910 \qquad N = 364$$

R_L = logged number of registrants, and all else is as in Equation 3.2.

This model also fits the data quite well. Again, the acceleration of Perón's vote is shown as one moves from smaller to larger places. Absolute residual analysis at the provincial level gives results which by now are familiar: the suburbs of the Federal Capital provide an excess of 31,000 Perón votes, Tucumán an excess of 19,000 votes, and Córdoba a deficiency of 26,000. Also deficient here is the Federal Capital, low by more than 12,000 votes. In relative terms, the pattern is much the same. The suburbs of the capital and the province of Tucumán are high (both by about 1.1 standard deviations), and Córdoba is low (−1.0 standard deviations). Finally, at the county level, the dramatic absolute surpluses in Perón's vote are found almost entirely in the suburbs of the Federal Capital, in Rosario, and in Tucumán. The dramatic deficits are in the capitals of the provinces of Buenos Aires and Córdoba.

As a next step, one could introduce dummy variables for the provinces in one or all of these regression models. Such a procedure would enhance the statistical explanation of the data, but it would not enhance their substantive explanation. What we want to know is which features of the pertinent provinces or counties are producing unusual levels of Perón support. Introduction of dummy variables would not answer that question; indeed, such variables would not even provide at this point bases for strong inferences. A more fruitful step is to turn to more meaningful variables.

The pair of variables central to our theoretical outlook, and to previous explanations of Perón's 1946 success, are "workers" and "migrants." The 1947 census, however, does not offer neat operational versions of those variables. "Migrant," as the census defines the term, is a category for males, including those under voting age, who at some point in their lives have moved out of (and in 1947 resided outside of) the province in which they were born—not those who have moved within the same province. Thus, within the huge province of Buenos Aires, there could have been (and undoubtedly was) a good deal of migration that was not registered in the census measure. Although it is probably true that within-province migrants in most instances must have settled in the same locations as between-province migrants, there is obvious imprecision in the numbers available to us and hence some further loss of ability to speak of the behavior of individuals as opposed to the behavior of counties. The problem of underage males seems less severe. We doubt that many children were in the wave of migration from the countryside. Those seeking work probably did not bring their families. Although there certainly must have been teenage job seekers (again, settling in the same locations as their older counterparts), we can do nothing to identify their numbers and must treat them simply as an error factor in any estimates of individual behaviors. Altogether, there are about 1.5 million people in our migrant category.

The category "worker" also presents a problem. The census counts are divided into agricultural, industrial, and commercial workers of two kinds, *obreros*—who can be thought of as manual laborers—and *empleados*—who can be thought of as all other workers, ranging from street vendors and messengers to clerks and white-collar workers. *Obreros* outnumber *empleados* roughly three million to one million. Within economic sectors, the numbers of *obreros* are not wildly different (.79 million in agriculture, 1.14 million in industry, and 1.07 million in commerce); however, the ratios of *obreros* to *empleados* vary greatly: 40:1 in agriculture, 8:1 in industry, and 5:4 in commerce. Relative (to population size) numbers of *empleados* from one sector do covary strongly with relative numbers of *obreros* from that same sector (and needless to say, absolute numbers of each even more so). Especially with units the size of counties, as here, the two groups can be expected to be concentrated in the same places. The covariance between commercial *obreros* and industrial *obreros* is slightly less pronounced, though still strong.

Separating the effects of highly correlated variables is an uncertain enterprise in ecological analysis. In the present case, most of the industrial workers live in the same locations as the commercial workers. However, the data make it clear that there were exceptions, most notably in the suburbs of the Federal Capital. Here one finds an extraordinarily high number of industrial workers. Otherwise the suburbs are much like the Federal Capital itself in terms of proportions of secondary and tertiary workers. Both locations are distinctive when compared with the rest of the nation.

Further complication comes from the fact that in the Federal Capital's suburbs, where industrial workers were so very numerous, migrants were also concentrated. Moreover, the overlap here is at the *individual* level: workers and migrants were very often the same people. The correlation between the numbers of migrants and industrial workers is .91. Of course, some migrants did not find work, and perhaps more commonly, some workers were not migrants. Still, the overlap makes it clear once again that we will not in this analysis be able to comment on how migrants as a group voted or on how workers as a group voted. At best, we will be able to say that at the margin—that is, with the overlap set aside— migrants or workers contributed more or less to Perón's success.

From this point forward, we take the registration model (Equation 3.3) as our baseline. The effects of other variables are tested in elaborations of that model. In other words, given the obvious point that Perón's vote is heavily dependent on numbers of registrants (that is, given the baseline), we now ask what factors other than sheer size will account for the support he received. From the outset we were sensitive to the potential for multicollinearity problems. Getting a little ahead of our findings, we can say here such problems did not undermine our analysis.

We begin with a model which goes to the heart of the debate about Perón's initial following. The model includes the all-important migrants and the largest of the worker categories, industrial *obreros*. This type of worker plays most prominently in previous explanations of Peronism. In contrast, agricultural *obreros,* cast into a patron-client network, have never been thought an important element in Perón's initial movement (except in Tucumán, where they also work the sugar refineries). The category *empleados* includes such a hodgepodge of different types of workers, significant numbers of them in a position to aspire to middle-class status, that it almost defies predictions about political behavior. The effect of commercial workers will be assessed later. The estimates for the model are:

$$(3.4) \quad P_L^* = -.43 + .83R_L + .11M_L + .10IO_L$$
$$ (5.5) \quad (22.1) \quad (4.0) \quad (4.1)$$

$$R^2 = .924 \quad N = 358$$

where M_L = migrants (logged), IO_L = industrial *obreros* (logged), and all else as in Equation 3.3.[46]

All coefficients are significant, and the explained variance is slightly increased from Equation 3.3. Given this model, one might argue that migrants (at the margin) supported Perón to about the same degree as industrial *obreros* (again, at the margin). However, this model is incomplete. It should also be noted that the number of migrants who were not industrial *obreros* was undoubtedly much greater than the number of industrial *obreros* who were not migrants. (There was a total of 1.5 million migrants and 1.1 industrial *obreros*.) Thus even though the relative numbers look comparable, the absolute numbers still favor the migrants.

What about the other worker categories? Equation 3.5 presents weighted regression results with the number of agricultural *obreros* and the combined number of commercial *obreros* and *empleados*— there seemed to be no clear basis for distinguishing between these two nearly equal blocs in the commercial sector—in the model.

$$(3.5) \quad P_L^* = -.52 + .85R_L + .12M_L + .14IO_L$$
$$ (6.4) \quad (16.0) \quad (4.5) \quad (5.4)$$
$$ + .03AO_L - .08CW_L$$
$$ (2.4) \quad\quad (1.9)$$

$$R^2 = .923 \quad N = 358$$

where AO = agricultural *obreros*, CW = all commercial workers, and all else as in Equation 3.4.

The results suggest again that migrants and industrial workers had roughly equal relative roles in Perón's success, that agricultural workers had a very small positive impact, and that commercial workers actually had a negative effect. There were many signs of inadequacy in the specification used for this model, however, most notably strong provincial effects which were not included. Upon further inspection of the data, we found that the averaging of worker and migrant effects across all observations obscured some dramatic differences from province to province. For example, when we went back to residuals from the baseline model (in which registration is the sole predictor), we found that the correlation of migrants with those residuals is +.69 for the suburbs of the Federal Capital and +.36 for the remainder of Buenos Aires province, but only +.15 for the Federal Capital itself. With respect to industrial workers the correlation is +.67 for the suburbs and +.47 for the Federal Capital, but only +.23 for the remainder of Buenos Aires. With respect to commercial workers, no correlation of consequence is found except for the suburbs of the Federal Capital, where it is +.51. And, finally, agricultural workers have no significant impact except in Tucumán, where the correlation reaches +.61.

When the residuals from the baseline model are regressed on the number of industrial workers, province by province, differences in intercept and slope are quite remarkable. For example, the intercept for the Federal Capital is very low, −3.95, and the slope is +0.89. The intercept for Córdoba is also quite low, −3.0, and the slope is +0.60. For the capital suburbs the figures are −0.39 and +0.38. Similar provincial differences occur when number of migrants is the independent variable.

These coefficients can be no more than illustrative, since the models are misspecified, but they serve admirably in this regard. It is clear that the final model in this examination of Peronist support must include terms for those provinces which are in one way or another peculiar. Ideally we would like to have access to additional variables which might permit specification of the substantive bases for these peculiarities, but such variables are not to be found in our data base. And we cannot even construct useful interaction terms in these data due to distributional problems. Except for Buenos Aires, the observations for any single province are so few that we effectively would end up with dichotomies; the distinction between a score of one and a score of three when 95 percent of the cases are scored zero is lost. Hence, although dummy variables are less than ideal, they are needed here to represent particular provinces in the overall model.

Prior to examining the provincial effects, we undertook a county-level ecological analysis in the tradition of French political geography.[47] Using six key demographical variables, we clustered counties which closely matched one another—using a chi-square test—on these six counts. The result was a taxonomy of counties which provided for analysis of the Peronist response by demographic/economic county types. The clustering had points of great intuitive appeal. For example, all of the capital cities of the smaller provinces clustered together in this exercise. What the clustering did not yield, however, was much of a contribution to an explanation of Peronist voting. In a regression analysis using these clusters (as dummy variables) we found the statistical power of the typology to fall substantially below the statistical power of simple provinces (also as dummy variables). In other words, we found that socioeconomic ecology was less important than political boundaries in Perón's 1946 victory.

The final model is presented in Equation 3.6, with dummies included for five provinces which, on a strictly empirical basis, were determined to be significant contributors to the overall statistical explanation of Peronist voting.

$$(3.6) \quad P_L^* = -.56 + .88R_L + .12M_L + .07IO_L + .10TUC$$
$$ (7.9) \quad (26.1) \quad (5.3) \quad (3.0) \quad (3.8)$$

$$ - .09CAT - .08FC - .11CDB - .16CRN$$
$$ (2.2) \quad (5.0) \quad (6.1) \quad (6.4)$$

$$R^2 = .939 \quad N = 358$$

TUC = Tucumán, CAT = Catamarca, FC = Federal Capital, CDB = Córdoba, CRN = Corrientes, and all else is as in Equation 3.5.

In this final model, the impact of migrants on Perón support is significantly higher than that of industrial workers. This difference plays into a difference in absolute numbers—1.5 million migrants versus 1.1 million industrial workers—to give reasonably strong support to our contention that migrants played a special role in the emergence of charisma in 1946 Argentina. That is not to say the industrial workers were not important. Let us emphasize again that many migrants were industrial workers and vice versa. Disentangling the two groups in any final sense is beyond the reach of our data and techniques. The evidence at hand, however, does indicate that at the margin, the migrants played a special part.

Some reasonable hypotheses can be advanced about why particular provinces are special in this model. Córdoba and the Federal Capital were longtime Radical strongholds. A newly emergent charismatic movement must find penetration of any population more difficult if that population has developed partisan attachments and political habits. Our speculation about Corrientes and Catamarca focuses more on ad hoc political arrangements made by local elites, involving not so much a partisan buffer to Perón's enticements as a personalist buffer: the traditional patron still influenced his clients in such smaller and less modern settings. Finally, we consider Tucumán. We believe the extraordinary response to Perón in this remote province came from the sugar workers, who were organized and ready when Perón emerged, and who responded to his worker initiatives and agrarian reform promises accordingly. (In fact, these workers went on strike when Perón was arrested on October 12, and demonstrated their support in the streets until his dramatic return on October 17.) Recall the unique correlation of agricultural workers in Tucumán with the residuals from the baseline model cited above. All this gives us some confidence in the contention that these sugar workers made the behavior of this province special.

A Per Capita Digression

As noted earlier, regression models using raw data are unconventional in ecological analysis. Much more common are investigations which use per capita data so that population size, the common element in virtually all of the variables, can be eliminated as an explanatory factor. Also noted earlier, however, were reasons not to do this. In the present case we were especially interested in preserving the original (though logged) numbers. Our "raw data" approach was possible only because multicollinearity did not undermine the analysis. Although we prefer the raw data analysis, it is useful to replicate that analysis with per capita data in order to test our findings from this more conventional angle. In so doing, we have opted to use the same denominator for all variables: the number of registrants in each county. Except in the Federal Capital, where some naturalization of foreign-born males occurred, this should closely approximate the number of Argentine-born males, eighteen and over, in each county. Note that use of this denominator is not equivalent to the earlier weighting by the same variable. In fact, in developing this ratio model it became obvious that WLS again was required. (The weight which produced constant variance in the residuals was equal to the number of registrants in each county.) The full model estimated with percentaged variables is:

$$(3.7) \quad P^* = .22 + .07R_L - .09C_L + .11M_L + .10IO_L$$
$$(4.1) \quad (6.6) \quad (3.8) \quad (6.1) \quad (5.9)$$

$$- .07FC - .09CDB + .07TUC - .09CRN$$
$$(6.5) \quad (7.1) \quad (4.1) \quad (7.1)$$

$$R^2 = .321 \quad N = 358$$

P^* is the percentage voting for Perón; C_L is the percentage, logged, of commercial workers; M_L is the percentage, logged, of migrants; IO_L is the percentage, logged, of industrial workers; and all else is as in Equation 3.6.

These results are quite similar to those from the component models. Both migrants and industrial workers have significant effects, with the former having a slightly greater impact. (And recall that this impact is further magnified by the much larger number of migrants.) Commercial workers again (at the margin) depress Perón's vote share. Except for Catamarca, the same provinces exhibit the same kinds of special effects. This equation captures about a third of the variance in Perón support.

A Simulation Postscript

In testing the relative contributions of industrial workers and migrants to early Peronism, we used one other technique in our analysis of the county data. A computer program was written to build aggregations of counties so that on any single specified variable there would be essentially no variance. On all other variables, however, variance would remain. The program would pull from the set of counties additional units until the cluster had the specified number of, say, migrants. Then that cluster would be set aside and a new one begun, and so on until all clusters that could be so assembled had been. This could be done at various levels, from that specified by the single largest county in terms of migrants on up. But whatever the level, the point was the same: to build clusters which had essentially no variance first in numbers of migrant and then later in numbers of industrial workers. The findings were straightforward and complementary to those given above: invariably, the relationship between industrial workers and the Peronist response, though pronounced, was not as great as that between migrants and the Peronist response.

Discussion

In these analyses two important points stand out. First, Peronism was especially strong in urban locations, most notably in the suburbs of the Federal Capital. This is no surprise: it was in such places, after all, that the massive demonstrations, first during Perón's imprisonment and later during the presidential campaign, occurred. Moreover, it was in such places that desperate conditions set the stage for the coming of a savior. The second point speaks to the question of who, within these settings, the Peronists were. What sectors of Argentine society spawned this movement? Our theory suggests that migrants should have played a special role. Cut off from their rural roots, scrambling to get bread, unsure of any future—migrants would be ripe, ready to respond to a leader they could believe in. Our findings are supportive of this interpretation, but they also point to the importance of industrial workers. The difficulty here is that we are working with highly imperfect measures and we are measuring the Peronist response at the margin. Our evidence so far is important, but not conclusive. We will add substantially to the evidence in Chapter 4. Before that, however, we turn to the small-unit data set described at the outset of this chapter.

Social and Political Ecology within the Federal Capital

Recall that the data for this part of our analysis come from 209 *circuitos* (or precincts) within the Federal Capital. For these units, the 1946 voting data are matched with socioeconomic characterizations of the units based upon 1959 data. (These characterizations are of value here because of the demonstrated socioeconomic status stability of the units during the period from 1946 to 1959.)[48] Also available for this analysis are data on the immediately prior voting behavior of each precinct.

Our dependent variable is the percentage of the total vote received by Perón. In our set of precincts, the support for Perón was normally distributed, with a mean of 51 percent (2 points under the figure for the Federal Capital as a whole) and a range from 22 to 73 percent. The first regression equation tested the effects of three socioeconomic status (SES) variables on the Perón response: percentage in blue-collar occupations, percentage in professional and business occupations, and percentage in white-collar occupations. Because the last had no impact of consequence (or of statistical significance) on the dependent variable, a new equation was estimated with only two SES factors. Here are the OLS results:

$$(3.8) \quad P^* = 47.0 - .54PB + .42BC$$
$$(21.9) \quad (8.2) \quad (9.8)$$
$$R^2 = .713 \quad N = 206$$

PB is the percentage of the voters in professional and business occupations, and BC is the percentage in blue-collar occupations.

More than 70 percent of the variance in Perón support is captured by this model. The class basis of the vote in the Federal Capital seems plain here. However, strictly speaking, one can only conclude that *places* with different social makeups behaved very differently in responding to Perón. The professional and business locations yielded comparatively few votes for him and the blue-collar locations comparatively many.

No other variable which could be used to characterize further the social ecology of these precincts had a significant effect on the Perón vote share. However, another approach was to examine Perón's support on the basis of political ecology. Our special interest was in the question of the leftist response to Perón. The Federal Capital had developed Socialist parties of consequence in the 1920s and 1930s. Did those areas having a strong Socialist vote in the 1942 election respond positively to Perón in 1946? Among our 209 precincts the average Socialist vote in 1942 was 30 percent; the range was from 18 to 51 percent. The results of this test and a similar test for the rightist alliance in 1942, the *Concordancia,* are:

$$(3.9) \quad P^* = 83.3 - .36S - .94C$$
$$ (14.1) \quad (3.1) \quad (7.6)$$

$$R^2 = .226 \quad N = 206$$

Here S = percentage Socialist and C = percentage *Concordancia.*

It is no surprise to find that those areas which gave support to a distinctly upper-class alliance in 1942 did not turn around and support Perón in 1946. It might be thought more curious, however, that areas where the Socialist vote was strong were not areas responding to Perón. Recall, however, that the Socialist leaders themselves did not support him, and the Communist leaders painted him as another Hitler or Mussolini. To the extent that such leaders could direct the vote, they urged support for the Unión Democrática alternative. Moreover, we must ask who the Socialists were. It turns out that the Socialist vote in 1942 had no clear class basis in its precinct vote. Regression of that vote on the three social ecology variables showed that the impacts of the percentage of white-collar, of blue-collar, and of professional/business voters were almost equally weak in predicting Socialist support. It was Peronism, not socialism, which brought a strong class basis to politics in the Federal Capital—and, for that matter, to Argentina as a whole.

Conclusions

Charismatic bonding depends on the fit between the attributes of a would-be leader and the desperate needs of prospective followers. This desperation, fed by diminished self-efficacy feelings and by fears of malignancy in the environment, makes seekers of its victims—seekers for explanations and seekers for help. Although some can find peace purely in ideology, more seem to find it with a savior (who may or may not offer a coherent ideology in the bargain).

In this chapter we have focused upon seekers in the 1946 Argentine context. Our theoretical argument, offered in Chapter 1, emphasized the importance of crisis, especially economic crisis, in setting the stage for Perón's bonding with a mass following. There had been such a crisis in Argentina. Between 1938 and 1944 the rural economy all but collapsed. We speculated that in the aftermath of that depression, those displaced from rural life and flooding into the *villas miserias* spotted around Argentina's commercial and industrial centers, principally the Federal Capital, would be prime candidates for bonding with a savior. Hence, we predicted that these migrants would be the most crucial social element in the birth of Peronism. This is not to say that others would not be significant sources of electoral support. Surely many established workers who had benefited from Perón's time in the Labor Ministry would have found him worthy. And the nonmigrant poor undoubtedly identified with and responded to the candidate who made them his cause. But the charismatic bond with Perón, in our view, was rooted in the migrants.

With this in mind, we looked for a special relationship in our data between migrants and Peronist support. The rival hypothesis was that early Peronism was a simple class-based phenomenon in which migration played no special role. Our measures are less than ideal, but they tell a consistent story nonetheless. Contrasted with industrial workers, and even allowing for various contextual effects, migrants did indeed have a special impact on Perón's 1946 vote. In the next chapter we take up the matter of seekers again, but instead of aggregate data we use survey evidence, and instead of 1946 we consider 1965.

★ 4 ★

Dispersion of the Charismatic Response

This chapter takes up the evolution of the charismatic bond.[1] Our theoretical view of charismatic evolution, presented in Chapter 1, identifies two stages: the development of structure and the dispersion of the charismatic response. In Chapter 2 we summarized how each stage appeared to unfold in the eyes of contemporary observers, as reported in newspapers and later in historical accounts. In what follows, we will present empirical analysis which treats the second stage of the process. In specific terms, we ask: twenty years after the formation of the charismatic bond, and ten years after Perón was forced into exile, what is left of the relationship with his erstwhile followers? Do devoted followers remain? If so, which ones? Have some transferred their loyalty to secondary leaders or to an organization? If so, which ones? Before turning to the analysis, however, we need to describe our data and the ways in which they have been utilized.

Data and Measurement

Our data are derived from interviews with a stratified sample of adult Argentines living in towns with populations of 2,000 or more.[2] The details of the original investigator's sampling procedures are available elsewhere.[3] Three points about the data should be underscored here. First, the 2,013 interviews were completed late in 1965, a decade after Perón was removed from power and two decades after his dramatic appearance in Argentine politics. Second, in the omnibus survey, questionnaire items probing the character of the respondents' feelings toward both Perón and his movement were relatively few in number. Third, the data are cross-sectional, obviously a limitation in any study of a dynamic process. One would like to have the kind of time-series survey data that would speak more directly to the hypotheses about change treated in Chapter 1. To require such data for the systematic testing of ideas about political dynamics, however, would mean that almost all such ideas would go untested. The little time-series data that is available, focused almost entirely on the United States and Western Europe in only the last few decades, cannot begin to capture the range of dynamic political phenomena of importance to political science. Of course none of this would matter if there were no way to examine change systematically except through time-series data, but such is not the case. This is a point much misunderstood. Time-series data, like all data, cannot prove a hypothesis; they can at best be compatible with it. One can specify expectations about how a process might unfold and then look to the data for support or disconfirmation. It is, of course, true that time-series data are stronger than cross-sectional data in such investigations, but it is not true that cross-sectional data are in some way inappropriate. The same testing of expectations can occur; support or disconfirmation can be forthcoming; the hypothesis weathers the test or it does not; and then one gets on with the business of devising another test.

Our first concern, in terms both of measurement and of theory, was to test the separability of the mass response to Perón on the one hand (what we call the "Personalist" response) and to the Peronist movement on the other (the "Organization" response). In particular, we sought verification in the data of two distinct Peronist tendencies. Various tests, using first cluster analysis and then factor analysis, indicated clearly that the collective response was in fact separable: those items dealing explicitly with Perón himself cohere in one fashion and those dealing with the Peronist movement in quite another. (Moreover, in validating this difference, we found that the "Personalist" and "Organization" sets of variables are distinctive in their relationships with external variables as well.) That is not to say that there is no overlap; a number of respondents clearly were attached both to the man and to the movement.

Ultimately we settled on a factor analytic version of the two measures, using an orthogonal rotation to maximize the distinctiveness of each. The results, along with the relevant marginal distributions, are presented in Table 4.1. It can be seen there that the factor loadings of the definitive items are both high and quite differentiated.

These results are for our purposes eminently suitable. We have one measure representing the Argentine public's response to Perón himself and another measure representing its response to Peronism. In the highest rankings of the first are respondents very supportive of Perón but lukewarm to the movement, and in the highest rankings of the second, respondents very supportive of the movement but actually somewhat negative in their feelings for the man.[4] In other words, at the positive extremes of these two measures are the two types of followers of primary interest.

Missing from the empirical definition of the Personalist dimension is direct evidence of emotional intensity. However, two types of evidence suggest that our most consistent Personalists were extremely strong in their emotional attachment to Perón. First, there was at the time of the survey virtual unanimity among journalists and social scientists concerned with Argentine politics that Perón continued to be the object of adoration and devotion for a substantial number of Argentine citizens. The exact numbers were debated, of course, but that they were very large seemed beyond argument.[5] That being the case, it would seem that devoted followers (who were not also devoted followers of the movement) would be located at the highest levels of our Personalist measure.

The second type of evidence suggesting that our consistent Personalists had an intense relationship with Perón comes from the distribution of the full sample of respondents on the Personalist measure. Weber tells us that charismatic followers are set apart from ordinary citizens by their extraordinary intensity of feeling. This

Table 4.1 Types of Peronism: Rotated factor matrix.

| Variables | % of Answers | | Loadings on Factor | | Commun- |
	Pro	Con	1[a]	2[b]	ality
Would vote for Perón[c]	18	55	.89	.20	.84
Wants Perón as presidential candidate[c]	21	54	.75	.13	.57
Would vote for Perón[d]	20	49	.74	.32	.66
Return Perón to power	21	60	.65	.43	.60
Return Perón to Argentina	26	50	.64	.47	.63
Peronist acts since 1955	26	49	.46	.48	.45
Peronist party identification[e]	16	30	.41	.36	.30
Admires Peronist leaders	19	70	.37	.33	.24
Supports Peronist candidates	37	46	.36	.71	.65
World figure most admired[d]	8	37	.30	.14	.14
Who harmed Argentina most[d]	46	34	.30	.48	.32
Supports goals of Bloc 62	23	18	.21	.48	.27
Supports Justicialist candidates	36	45	.19	.76	.61
Supports Bloc 62 candidates	46	32	.13	.62	.40

a. Personal or concentrated charisma.
b. Organizational or dispersed charisma.
c. Perón's name mentioned in the question.
d. Perón's name had to be volunteered.
e. "Con" answers indicate identification with a non-Peronist party.

suggests that such followers are not simply at the high end of a normal distribution of emotional involvement but are in fact "outliers" in such a distribution. As can be seen in Figure 4.1, this is borne out on our Personalist measure. The Organization measure, though a bit flat, approximates normality; the Personalist measure

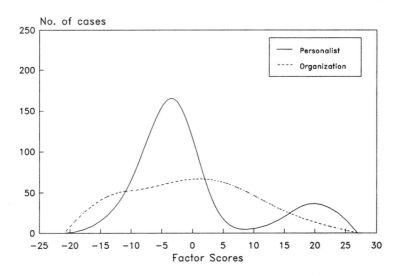

Figure 4.1 Distributions of Perón and Peronism.

is highly skewed to the left and clearly bimodal. One peak is found at the point of slight opposition and the other, smaller peak at the extreme positive end.

This latter distribution suggests that perhaps as many as three hundred of our respondents exhibit a special bond with Perón; but to make the case even stronger, in the following analysis we will treat only the one hundred cases at the very top of this distribution, comparing them with a similarly "pure" group of one hundred taken from the highest scores on the Organization dimension. Note that this procedure does not constitute sampling on a dependent variable, nor is it a matter of throwing out cases in the middle of a distribution. What we analyze below is not a single dimension with supporters of the man at one extreme and supporters of the movement at the other extreme, but rather two separate distributions with all 2,013 respondents arrayed on each. What we have done is to isolate two pure types, one at the extreme positive end of each distribution. These types, not the population as a whole, are the objects of our analysis.

Throughout the analysis it must be kept in mind that our differentiation between the two types of Peronists does not involve formal membership of any kind. Neither membership in the Peronist Party, nor membership in the Justicialist movement, nor membership in a Bloc 62 trade union is involved in this differentiation. Attachment to the "organization," like attachment to the man, is entirely affective and symbolic.

Of the remaining measures, relatively little need be said at this point. Basically there are three kinds: individual items, simple additive indices, and weighted additive indices. The first includes several demographic characteristics; the second includes several two-item attitude measures in which the indices were constructed by summing the standardized scores of the defining items. The third includes factor analytic measures of socioeconomic class and of several political attitudes.[6] To facilitate presentation, all measures have been standardized, with means set equal to zero and variance equal to one.

Since we found what appeared to be an agreement bias in a battery of agree-disagree attitude items, we constructed an indicator of this tendency and used it as a control when these items were used in our analysis. Thus, in such instances we used the residual of an agree-disagree item rather than the item itself. This had the effect of discounting the meaning of an agree response when the individual respondent had agreed with virtually all the propositions in the battery.[7]

In the following analysis we examine the differential standing of our two types of Peronists with respect to a number of factors central to our argument about the dispersion of charisma. First we discuss those variables definitive of socioeconomic location; second we treat relevant psychological orientations; and finally we repeat these analyses for younger members of each type of Peronist. Discriminant analysis is used both to assess the importance of particular measures within relevant variable clusters and to determine the importance of the clusters as a whole.[8]

Socioeconomic Location

We argued in Chapter 1 that the dispersion of charisma is likely when figures subordinate to the leader come to be seen as independent sources of important material and/or psychic benefits. Put somewhat differently, dispersion is likely when followers come to feel that secondary leaders have taken the initiative in advancing their interests. This complex process depends upon many more factors than we can estimate within the data at our disposal; however, we can specify two necessary conditions, which in turn permit several *ceteris paribus* predictions about how the two faces of Peronism should be expected to appear in our 1965 observations.

The first requirement is that the individual follower be in a location which permits contact with, or at least awareness of, Organization leaders. Moreover, a location where contact is continuous rather than episodic, and direct rather than indirect, will provide the greatest opportunity for influence. In the decade following Perón's exile, such contact was concentrated in the nation's large urban centers, and especially in greater Buenos Aires. It was there that the Peronist movement was strongest, and it was there that its mobilization efforts, whether in struggles for economic benefits or in campaigns for national political office, were centered. One should expect the dispersion of Perón's charisma to have been most likely in such a setting.

Similar reasoning leads us to expect dispersion to be greater among respondents from union households. Given the Peronist domination of most trade unions, and given the post-1955 dominance of the Peronist movement by its union wing, union membership is likely to have brought about contact with Organization personnel. This expectation, however, is somewhat weakened by the existence of a number of unions led by non-Peronists.[9]

The second condition is the receipt of benefits which followers attribute to the Organization. If those with great need see no benefits flowing to them from the secondary leadership, one should not expect them to be weaned from a Personalist orientation— especially if that orientation is being nurtured and reinforced by idealized reminiscences about the past.

The benefits which between 1955 and 1965 could have been associated with the Peronist movement were primarily economic. Although gains in real wages were insubstantial during this period, this must be considered against a backdrop of rampant inflation in which merely "keeping up" was a heroic feat.[10] It was Perón's lieutenants, especially those in the trade unions, who were the most visible in the struggle to prevent the workers' conditions from deteriorating. We thus anticipated that where followers were at least holding their own, the dispersion of the charismatic response would be more likely—though by no means certain. Conversely, where followers had slipped back or had remained in poverty, the attractions of secondary leaders should have been minimal.

With these rather elementary predictions we turned to the data. In Table 4.2 we present the group means[11] and discriminant function coefficients for the socioeconomic location variables. The results are very much as expected. Looking first at the mean scores,

Table 4.2 Socioeconomic location.

Components	Discriminant Function Coefficients	Standardized Scores	
		Org.	Pers.
Greater Buenos Aires	.50	+26	−29
Union household	.19	+48	+11
Recent migration	.31	−06	+33
Small town residence	.11	−12	+27
Masculinity	.48	+40	−07
Summary class	.53	−32	−87
Interviewer appraisal		−18	−71
Subjective class		−42	−67
Occupation		−24	−50
Education		−24	−74
Group memberships correctly classified		71%	76%
Canonical correlation		.51	

we find that Organization followers are substantially more likely than are Personalists to come from greater Buenos Aires—they also surpass the nation as a whole in this respect—while the Personalists are well below the national norm. In addition, the Organization types are more likely than are Personalists to be found in union households, although both groups are above the overall average. Personalists stand out in terms of their small town origins and the recency of their migration. Finally, the mean scores on our summary class measure are also in keeping with our argument; the Personalists are found dramatically below the Argentine average, and substantially below Organization followers as well.[12] (These differences are not a function of disparate age distributions. For example, had Organization followers been quite young, their education level might simply have reflected the secular trend of education levels in Argentine society. In fact, the age distributions of our two groups are almost identical.)

The only real surprise in Table 4.2 is the proportion of women in the Personalist group. In general analyses of political involvement in Argentina we have found that men were invariably and substantially overrepresented. Why women should here be as highly represented as men—in fact, a bit *more* highly represented—is not clear. Several potential explanations come to mind: one might focus on the tie between Perón and his wife Evita, far and away the most visible and dramatic female political actor in Argentine history; another might place emphasis on the enfranchisement of women under Perón's leadership; still another might point to the sex appeal which is sometimes thought to characterize charismatic leaders.[13] Unfortunately, none of these possibilities can be tested in our data. However, this finding with respect to sex does strike us as eminently compatible with the locational perspective we have argued. Other things being equal, women in Argentina were certainly less likely than men to have contact with the personnel and propaganda of the Peronist movement.

The discriminant function coefficients give us a measure of the importance of each of our variables, with the effects of the others statistically controlled. It can readily be seen in Table 4.2 that differentiation of our two Peronist types depends primarily on residence in greater Buenos Aires, on class, and on sex. The importance of recent migration is somewhat smaller, though still significant, and that of union membership and small town residence smaller still. The discriminatory power of the entire set of variables is captured by the canonical correlation, here .51. Finally, figures describing the proportions correctly classified within each group are provided. Among the Personalists 76 percent are correctly classified on the basis of the function here defined; 71 percent of the Organization followers are so classified.[14]

These findings support the view that socioeconomic location is a significant factor in the dispersion of charisma. Two additional kinds of evidence also support our view of the importance of Organization contact. The first comes from further analysis of migration patterns, in which we found that the Organization followers were as likely to have moved at some point in their lives as were the Personalists, but their moves tended to come before Perón rose to power. The modal pattern for Personalists was to move after Perón's exile, a period in which the Organization followers were quite settled, even in comparison with the population as a whole. Again, both the stability of the Organization followers and the mobility of the Personalists affect (of course, in different directions) the probability of significant Organizational influence on them after 1955.

A second and more direct line of evidence deals with the respondents' knowledge of Peronist leaders. When asked their opinions of nine prominent Peronist lieutenants, 27 percent of the Personalist group had not heard of *any* of them, and another 35 percent had heard of only one. Comparable figures for the Organizationalists were 10 and 15 percent. That almost two-thirds of the Personalists would have such little awareness of the secondary figures of Peronism is rather dramatic evidence of their irrelevance for that group. Moreover, among the Personalists who expressed opinions on these Peronist leaders, more than half were invariant in their evaluations, leaving the impression that what was being tapped was more response-set than true judgment. Only one in five of the Organization followers who expressed an opinion showed this invariance. It seems quite clear that the secondary figures of Peronism did not have the same significance for our two groups.

A final measure relevant to the contact-benefits perspective on Organization influence—and to the dispersion of charisma—is the respondents' view of union political activities. As noted above, Peronist domination of the union movement was likely to make this in effect a question about the movement's activities. It requires only a small step to see in this attitudinal measure an indicator of benefits received: if one is favorably disposed toward union (that is, Peronist) activities it is probably because those activities have resulted in some measure of personal gain. To minimize possible circularity, we tested this with simultaneous controls for all the demographic features which significantly differentiate Personalist from Organization followers (including residence in union households). We found that the Organizationalists were significantly more favorably disposed toward union political activities than were Personalists, although the latter were themselves more positive than the general public. The relevant standardized scores are $+.47$ and $+.24$.

It might be thought that age cohort would be a significant factor in predicting the nature of the Peronist attachment in these respondents, with the old hanging on to past Personalist feelings and the young embracing the Organization sentiment. There is evidence from American party-identification studies for such cohort-driven changes in collective response.[15] However, we believe that the process here is different from the process through which a party (or any other organization) loses appeal. The charismatic bond is for persons, young or old, who are seekers—who rely upon proxy control for dealing with crucial problems in their lives. In the present case there is no reason to believe that the young as a group would be free from such a need, and the old as a group be animated by it. Hence that the data showed no such distinction is not surprising. Instead, equal proportions of each group (20 percent) are drawn from the under-thirty population. Younger recruits were being drawn into each group, a point we will return to in discussing recruitment.

It seems clear that if dispersion of charisma is to occur, there must be visible individuals or roles that it can be dispersed to, and there must be some reason for dispersal to occur. In this case, where followers of Perón had little or no contact with the Peronist movement or where that contact seemed to produce no consequential change in the condition of their lives, one would not expect a transferal of allegiance and reverence from the man who had so dramatically changed their lives to the movement.

The Organization followers, in contrast, could gradually be weaned away from their earlier attachment to Perón and be brought to transfer loyalty to the movement and its personnel precisely because that movement had relevance to their circumstances. Perón may have continued as an object of reverence for many, especially during his first few years in exile, but as the initiatives of the movement pushed him more into the shadows of their day-to-day consciousness—a process which was neither sudden nor dramatic —Peronism was increasingly likely to become the stronger force.

Before leaving our examination of socioeconomic location as a determinant of charismatic dispersion, we must consider the possibility that irrespective of anything the movement might or might not have done, a general improvement in societal conditions could reduce societal stress and hence, with the passage of time, lessen mass receptivity to a strong leader. Certainly by 1965 there had been substantial improvement in the social and economic conditions of working-class Argentines, though as noted in Chapter 2, those gains came early and were unevenly distributed. We cannot disprove the contention that some erosion of the charismatic bond with Perón occurred not because of the initiatives attributed to the movement but because a general amelioration of stressful conditions left some followers without the need for proxy control. But on balance, we tend to discount the importance of this objective change in producing the type of Peronist found in our movement group because it does not seem to have registered in the psychological outlook of that group. Recall that movement followers scored almost as low as the Personalists in terms of *subjective* social class. Hence we conclude that the efforts, symbolic and material, of the movement leadership were indeed important to the dispersion of charisma.

Attitudinal Differentiation

Thus far we have focused on the contextual factors involved in the dispersion of charisma. Now we turn to psychological factors. Using the same data-analytic techniques that were employed in the previous section, we explore differences between Personalists and their Organization counterparts with respect to three complex orientations toward political life. Two of them, self-efficacy and deference to authority, are central to our theory of the formation and maintenance of a charismatic bond; the third, left radicalism, is important to an alternative view of the appeal of Perón and Peronism.

Self-Efficacy

As argued in Chapter 1, negative conclusions about self-efficacy are crucial in setting the stage for charismatic bonding. When coping efforts fail and feelings of self-efficacy collapse, people desperately seek help, psychological as much as material, from a leader they trust and believe in. Maintenance of this charismatic bond also is tied to negative feelings about self and environment. Our expectation here is that Personalists, but not Organizationalists, would see their self-efficacy as very low.

Operational definitions of self-efficacy vary considerably from study to study. Ours includes three elements: a sense of being able to understand the relevant environment, a sense of control over relevant events, and a sense of responsiveness by the relevant environment. Because we are interested in the *lack* of self-efficacy we formulate each of the three in negative terms.

There is one important deficiency in our measures: each of the survey items available to us has a political or governmental referent. Although concerned with political charisma in this study, we do not believe that the most important environment for definition of self-efficacy is so remote.[16] More intimate environments and more directly personal objects of control would have been better referents for our purposes, but we are of course bound by the limits of secondary analysis.

The empirical presence of the three negative dimensions was established by factor analyzing ten items. A three-factor solution, capturing 55 percent of the total variance, was found to match nicely the expected dimensionality—and this was true regardless of the rotation employed. The results (using an orthogonal solution) are presented in Table 4.3. To construct the final indices, we used separate principal components analyses of the relevant item pools: Environmental Responsiveness, Understanding, and Control. As with our other indices, we went on to confirm that each measure exhibited an item cohesion with the Peronist subsets similar to that within the sample as a whole.

We anticipated that the figures on all three dimensions would be lower for Personalists than for either the Organization followers or the national sample. Inspection of the average standard scores in Table 4.4 reveals that this is indeed the case, although the difference is large only in the case of Understanding. Still, all three differences are statistically significant.

In comparison with the Organization followers and with the population as a whole, Personalists are less inclined to believe that they understand politics, more inclined to believe that the political environment is hostile, and thus less inclined to believe that they are efficacious in political life. This is what Bandura's theory would lead one to expect. Because the measures are far from ideal, we are not surprised by the less than dramatic strength of the findings.

Discriminant analysis confirms these findings in every respect. It also shows that the overall power (canonical correlation = .29) of

Table 4.3 Rotated factor matrix of self-efficacy variables.

	Factor Scores		
Variables	Env. Resp.	Under-standing	Control
Expects unfair treatment from government officials	.642	.008	.072
Expects government officials would ignore complaints	.791	.014	.063
Expects unfair treatment from police and courts	.737	.021	.049
Expects police and courts would ignore complaints	.794	.011	.085
Average man cannot understand politics	.004	.429	.089
Respondent does not understand politics	.022	.761	.075
Has little citizen influence	.065	.052	.523
Could do nothing to prevent passage of unfair law	.001	.079	.335
Votes do not decide how the government is run	.102	.129	.217
Does not have any say in government	.017	.150	.413
Common variance explained	61%	25%	14%

the self-efficacy factors—as measured here—is well below that of socioeconomic location (see Table 4.4). Interestingly, although 71 percent of the Personalists are correctly classified in the analysis, this is true of only 50 percent of the Organizationalists. The latter group is widely scattered along the dimension defined by the discriminant function, thus permitting a taxonomic success rate no better than chance. We will come back to this point.

Table 4.4 Self-efficacy.

Components	Discriminant Function Coefficients	Standardized Scores	
		Org.	Pers.
Understanding	.87	+30	−22
Environmental Responsiveness	.40	−11	−37
Control	.22	−04	−20
Group memberships correctly classified		50%	71%
Canonical correlation		.29	

Deference to Authority

Social scientists have only scant knowledge of the importance of either contextually- or personality-based deference to authority in political leader-follower relationships. Here we test only the view, elaborated in Chapter 1, that a need for proxy control—one predicted consequence of a collapse in self-efficacy—inspires deference to authority. The anticipation is that Personalists will be distinctive in such deference.

We employ three quite different indicators of deference. The first is a single survey item, familiar to students of authoritarianism, which asks if a few strong leaders would do more for the country than all the laws and talk. This item taps an explicit preference in political life, and it may well have been interpreted by respondents as a question about Perón. The second measure, the index of acquiescence described earlier, is more general, with no focus on government or politics. We do not wish to argue, and have no reason to believe, that the disposition toward acquiescence is deeply rooted in the psyche and beyond the reach of events; it simply captures a behavioral deference in the interview situation. Finally, the third measure, also a single item, asks whether or not duty to the state should take precedence over individual concerns. With the state referent, this measure may have been taken to be an inquiry about the regime then in power. Alternatively, it may have been seen as a question about patriotism. With these possibilities in mind, we went into the analysis with no expectation of how this measure might relate to Personalist or Organization attachments. Results are presented in Table 4.5.

Looking first at the "strong leaders" scores, one can see that the Personalists are indeed likely to endorse the proposition that such leaders are needed, and that the position of the Organizationalists does not differ appreciably from that of the nation as a whole. Because this first finding may have underlying it an equation of the term "strong leaders" with Perón himself, we are much more impressed with the second, which is that while those attached to the movement are well above the national average in acquiescence, the Personalists are much higher still. Thus generalized behavioral deference has clear importance in differentiating our two groups. On the third measure, however, we find that sense of duty to the state does not predict well. Neither Peronist group is far from the position of the nation as a whole, and it is the Organizationalists who are on the positive side.

The discriminant function coefficients reproduce these findings.

Table 4.5 Deference to authority.

Components	Discriminant Function Coefficients	Standardized Scores	
		Org.	Pers.
Strong leaders	.72	−09	+31
Acquiescence	.63	+24	+60
State duty	.27	+11	−11
Group memberships correctly classified		59%	65%
Canonical correlation		.29	

Both the strong leaders item and the acquiescence measure contribute strongly to the differentiation of the two Peronist types. The canonical correlation (.29) is exactly the same as that obtained for self-efficacy. There is somewhat greater success in classifying the Organizationalists (59 percent versus 50 percent) and somewhat less for the Personalists (65 percent versus 71 percent).

Overall, the differences found here lend weight to the common-sense view that deference to *personalized* authority is indeed an element in maintenance of the bond with a charismatic leader. Those lacking that deference (for whatever reason) are better prepared for a dispersion of their response from the charismatic figure to secondary leaders and the organization itself. Again, we do not claim that personality features are involved here. It could be that more enduring aspects of psychic makeup are relevant, but it could also be that events are more important.

Left Radicalism

Previous research offers us a clear basis for expecting self-efficacy and deference to authority to influence the bond between a charismatic leader and his or her following. The basis for anticipating the importance of the "left radical" variables discussed in this section is less plain. One point to remember is that while president (between 1946 and 1955), Perón was in no sense a radical leftist. Also, there was no appreciable leftist current in Peronist unions prior to 1955, though such a sector did come into being following military intervention in the unions in 1955.[17] One might thus speculate that any Peronists who embraced left radical views would find themselves in the classic condition of cognitive imbalance.[18] That is, the bond with a nonleftist leader and the attachment to a leftist ideology would be incompatible. One way to resolve this— and balance theory contends that resolution of such imbalance, if recognized, is crucial—would be the diminution of feelings for the leader.

We include three multiple-item indices in the left radicalism set. They vary in terms of their degrees of radicalism, their distance from the positions taken by Perón while president, and their expressive versus instrumental character. The first is support for substantial redistribution of wealth. This measure departs least from Perón's own position, although it does involve hypothetical policies that go beyond anything he actually did while in power. Of the three indices, this is clearly the one most likely to have elicited responses of an instrumental nature, since it speaks directly to material concerns.

The second index focuses on working-class militance. It measures the extent to which support for worker-sponsored presidential candidates exceeds that for candidates backed by elite groups (for example, big landowners, the Church, or business). Although class militance was sometimes a part of Perón's rhetoric as president, his actual policies were apparently designed to prevent class conflict. To the extent that his followers correctly perceived those policies and the beliefs that lay behind them, we would expect only moderately positive scores on this measure. We view this index as one likely to have produced a mixture of expressive and instrumental responses. Expression of candidate support, for example, may be tied to a relatively clear set of policy expectations, or it may represent a symbolic rejection or endorsement of particular parties, leaders, or social classes.

The third measure is the most radical of the set, and the most expressive. It indexes support for friendly relations with Communist nations. The measure is not related to support for candidates backed by the Argentine Communist Party and should not be considered a simple pro-Communist measure. Moreover, it should be remembered that in 1945 and 1946, Perón was bitterly attacked by the Argentine Communists and by the Soviet Union, which each considered him the Argentine version of a fascist leader.

The mean scores for these three indices, presented in Table 4.6, reveal several interesting points. The two groups are quite similar in their views toward redistributive economic policies, and are each substantially to the left of the national norm. On the other two indices the groups' differences are striking. The strong preference of Organization followers for worker-backed candidates contrasts

Table 4.6 Left radicalism.

Components	Discriminant Function Coefficients	Standardized Scores	
		Org.	Pers.
Communist contact	.83	+54	−07
Worker candidates	.43	+62	+20
Economic redistribution	.01	+45	+40
Group memberships correctly classified		48%	75%
Canonical correlation		.30	

with a much weaker, although still supportive, stance among Personalists. More remarkable still, with respect to contact with Communist nations, the Organizationalists are supportive whereas the Personalists are essentially like the population as a whole, strongly in opposition.

The discriminant function coefficients tell much the same story. Approval of contact with Communist nations is the most powerful predictor, followed by support for worker-backed candidates; attitudes toward redistributive policies make virtually no contribution. The canonical correlation is .30—almost the same as self-efficacy and deference to authority. Once again, the discriminant function is successful in classifying Personalists (75 percent) but not Organizationalists (48 percent).

We see, then, that the Organization group does take a comparatively radical leftist stance. The Personalists, however, are different. On the "bread and butter" redistribution issue they are as far left as the movement followers, but on worker candidates they are no more than lukewarm, and on the Communist contact index they are not on the left at all.

That the Organizational Peronists would tend toward leftist views may be a function of a variety of factors. To begin with, members of this group tended to occupy socioeconomic locations where the issues of the left were more likely to have been actively debated. Second, some leaders in the movement, especially within the "combative unions," themselves voiced radical views. Finally and probably most important, as we noted in Chapter 1, ideologies like that characterized here as "left radicalism" may provide an "understanding" of political life after a charismatic leader has for one reason or another left his flock behind.

In the pattern of Personalist scores we find what appears to be a strong instrumental strain running through their responses. They have little reason to be interested in symbolic leftism; policies which will actually deliver the goods engage their sympathies. Given their depressed economic circumstances, this is not at all surprising. Moreover, this type of leftism departs least from Perón's own, and thus their selectivity here is in keeping with their personalism.

Combined Attitudinal Effects

It was clear from the correlations we calculated among the three attitude functions that each was relatively independent of the others. In order to determine more precisely the individual and combined effects of the nine attitudinal measures, we entered them in a new discriminant analysis. We found that the coefficients from this grand discriminant function were almost exactly proportional to those presented in Tables 4.4, 4.5, and 4.6. The indices of strong leaders, acquiescence, understanding, and Communist contact remain the most powerful. Second, in keeping with the independence of the three functions, the canonical correlation between the nine-item function and Peronist identification rises to .47, much closer to the power of the socioeconomic location function. Finally, success in classification is increased: 78 percent of the Personalists and 65 percent of the Organizationalists are correctly assigned.

In summary, it can be seen that there are quite significant differences between Personalists and Organization followers with respect to the three types of psycho-political orientation we have considered. Of course, a variety of other attitudes may also be distinctively associated with one or the other group of Peronists. Our focus on self-efficacy, deference to authority, and left radicalism is not meant to suggest the absence of other relevant predispositions, but the three we have examined seem to us the most germane.

Combined Sociological and Psychological Effects

In order to test the relative strength of the psychological and sociological summary measures in explaining the dispersion of charisma, we undertake a final discriminant analysis. The two variates, attitudes and social location, are independent "variables" in this analysis, and group classification is the dependent variable. Note that this is not meant as a causal assessment; too much is happening *within* each variate for any causal specification to make sense. It is merely a means of specifying and weighing the independent effects of the dimensions developed in the previous analyses.

Our first concern is the relationship between these two variates. The correlation is .51. On the face of it, this is quite strong. Another test, however, shows just how dramatic the fit between the two variates really is. Remember that each of these variates represents a weighted set of variables, with the weighting in every case determined by the capacity of the variable involved to predict Peronist orientation. It is possible, using canonical correlation analysis, to re-weight the variables on both sides of this relationship. The canonical correlation is calculated in such a way as to assign weights on both sides simultaneously to maximize the capacity of each set to explain (statistically) the other. In other words, this re-weighting maximizes the correlation between sets. That maximum correlation turns out to be .61, only slightly higher than that between the above variates. In other words, the variates established by fitting Peronist orientation are correlated at nearly the highest possible level. Such a correlation means that the set of socioeconomic circumstance most predictive of Peronist orientation almost optimally "explains" the weighted set of attitudes most predictive of that same orientation.

$$(4.1) \quad PO^* = .36SE + .30P$$
$$(19.7) \quad (28.9)$$

$$R^2 = .322 \quad N = 205$$

The regression model to test the relative power of socioeconomic and psychological factors yields the following results, where PO* = Peronist orientation; SE = socioeconomic factors; P = psychological factors; the figures in parentheses are F statistics; R^2 = the coefficient of determination; and N = the number of observations.

From this analysis we can see that both socioeconomic and psychological factors have pronounced effects on Peronist orientation. The former is somewhat stronger than the latter, though given the weaknesses of the latter we are reluctant to draw any firm conclusions about the relative power of sociological and psychological explanations. The two factors are so strongly interrelated, no doubt with very complex causal intertwinings, that we are left with only one conclusion: both are important to this outcome.

Throughout this chapter we have argued that the Organization followers are those for whom the dispersion of charisma has taken place, that is, those who have transferred their loyalty from the original charismatic leader to his movement and perhaps its secondary leaders. The use of cross-sectional analysis does not allow us to *demonstrate* this, or any other, process. We thus have undertaken two tests, each of which leaves us reasonably comfortable with our inferences about the process of charismatic dispersion.

The first test involves examining a third group of Peronists—another group of one hundred respondents, this time those who are supportive, albeit to a lesser degree, of both Perón and the Organization. We would argue that these people, like the Organizationalists, have moved away from Personalism, but not as far. Their intermediate location in the dispersion process should then be associated with a similar intermediate position on our socioeconomic and attitude discriminant functions (which were constructed without reference to this mixed group).

The results of this test are as predicted. The mean score of the mixed Peronists is precisely on the zero point of the socioeconomic function and very near the zero point on the attitude function. Decomposition of the latter reveals that the small deviation from zero is almost entirely due to sympathy for the Organization position on a single measure, that of left radicalism.

The second assessment is based on the distributions of the two Peronist groups on the discriminant functions. As mentioned earlier, in every discriminant analysis we were more successful in classifying Personalists than Organizationalists. In a statistical sense, the explanation for this is that the scores of the former are clustered more tightly around their group centroid than are the scores of the latter. The variance of the Organizationalist scores is, on average, 54 percent greater than the Personalist variance. This statistical fact fits quite well with our argument that the Personalist group has maintained its original form of attachment to Perón, while the Organizational group has moved away from such an attachment. One should not expect this movement to begin for all followers at the same time, or for the rate of movement to be the same for everyone; hence one may predict that during the process of dispersion, those individuals departing from the original form of attachment will be spread relatively broadly along both the socioeconomic and the attitudinal continua. And that is exactly what we find, especially with regard to attitudes. A plot of the discriminant scores shows that the Personalists are relatively tightly clustered, while the Organizationalists are spread out from a point near the Personalist centroid all the way to the other end of the continuum.

Although these two results do not fully validate our process argument, they are certainly supportive of it. They substantially reduce the possibility that Organizationalists, rather than having evolved from Personalism, as we have argued, instead emerged as a new and completely separate variant of Peronism. And that possibility is further diminished by the absence of any age differential between the two groups.

Recruitment of New Blood

Within each of our Peronist groups we have some who were too young in 1945 to have been involved in the original process of charismatic bonding, persons who were "recruited" much later into either the Personalist or the Organization group. What sort of people were they? Was the social and psychological makeup of the recruits like that of their older counterparts, which would suggest stability within and constant differences between the two Peronist groups? Or was that makeup different, leading to variance within and a narrowing, or perhaps a widening, of differences between them?

We assumed that the intimate environmental conditions leading people to seek proxy control in political life would be much the same whether they were doing so in 1945 or in 1965. This is not to say, however, that the conditions for the country as a whole were similar. Nor does it mean that a movement could have sprung into existence in 1965 as it did in 1945. What was different in the early 1940s was that very large numbers of people had been thrown into the type of confusion and despair which undermines feelings of self-efficacy. There was a critical mass of citizens primed for the leadership of a seemingly heroic figure. After the original bonding between Perón and his following, even in exile he remained a beacon for the despairing. That such a beacon existed made 1965 crucially different from the early 1940s. But in addition, the country's economic conditions in 1965 were substantially improved over those of the earlier period. Displaced agricultural workers were no longer pouring into the cities. Real per capita gross domestic product was much higher.[19] There surely were those who were in personal crisis—and thus recruitable to Perón's banner—but the numbers were much smaller and the circumstances quite different.

With respect to the Organization young, our a priori reasoning took an obvious tack. Given both our argument and the distribution of our data along the discriminant function, we viewed the older Organizationalists as having gone through a process of leaving an earlier Personalist orientation: hence the spread of Organizationalists along the function, moving away from the Personalist centroid. The younger Organizationalists, we reasoned, should be like their older counterparts, but more so—that is, having little or no Personalist attachment to "overcome," they should be farther along that discriminant (dispersion) function.

Before turning to the evidence, we must insert an important caveat. The data speaking to this question of recruitment are much less firm than we would have liked. Using an age division point of thirty years, we find one-fifth of our original one hundred cases in each youth component. We therefore examine twenty cases of Personalist youth and about the same number of Organizationalist youth. Although these figures do not seem unrealistic in terms of population parameters (for example, these figures would translate into about 120,000 young adults in each wing of Peronism), they do illustrate the problem of using general population samples in analyses of important but small subgroups. The evidence presented below must be considered in that light. Our own view is that the persuasiveness sacrificed by the data in purely statistical terms is substantially recovered by two tests of adequacy: strong empirical patterns, and a clear fit with other sources of evidence.[20]

Socioeconomic Differences

In our groups of young Peronists we have individuals who were no more than ten years old, and in some cases were not even born, when Perón's initial bond with his following was formed in 1945. They were between eight and twenty years old when he was forced into exile. How does their socioeconomic makeup compare with that of their older counterparts?

The Personalist young and old were indeed much the same. It is true that the young were a bit poorer and a bit better educated, but the only striking difference had to do with recent migration, which was much more likely for the young than for the old (who were themselves well above the population average in terms of migration).

With respect to the Organizationalists, in most of the social and economic conditions of the old and young we found a reasonably close match. There was one astonishing exception: the young were of much higher social status, scoring even above the average for the Argentine population as a whole, while their older counterparts scored well below the average. In class terms, then, these young Organizationalists were very different indeed.

The major findings are presented in Figures 4.2 and 4.3. In

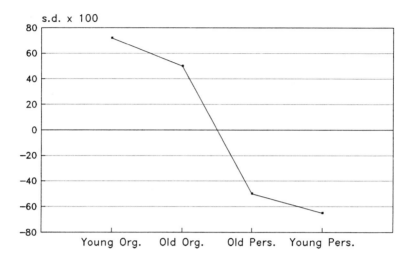

Figure 4.2 Age cohorts in charismatic dispersion: summary socioeconomic variate.

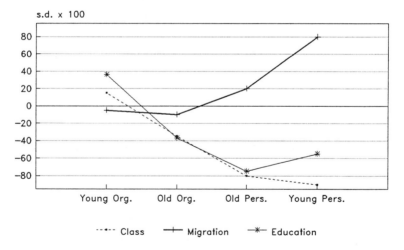

Figure 4.3 Age cohorts in charismatic dispersion: individual socioeconomic factors.

Figure 4.2 is the position of each group (young and old Personalist and young and old Organizationalists) on a summary socioeconomic measure, which is standardized across the two hundred Peronist cases to produce a mean of zero and a standard deviation of one. This measure, actually a canonical variate, was derived from the earlier discriminant function analysis in which weights were assigned to social and economic variables on the basis of their capacity to discriminate between Personalist and Organization Peronists. Age was not involved in that weighting process.

This summary measure shows that the two younger groups were even farther apart than their older counterparts—a finding that portends not stability or convergence but rather a growing gap between the two wings of Peronism. In their social foundations Peronists were coming to have less and less in common. The particulars in this growing gap are found in Figure 4.3. The factors most powerful in differentiating the newer recruits are recent migration, social class, and education. (Remember that these variables were standardized across the entire sample, permitting group scores to be compared with population averages as well as with each other.)

Psychological Differences

The attitudinal differences between young and old Personalists can quickly be summarized. The young felt slightly less able to understand politics (in spite of their higher educational level); they were much less likely to promise support to political candidates from the working class; they were appreciably more supportive of a strong leader; and they scored much higher on the measure of acquiescence to authority. To an even greater extent than their older counterparts, these young Personalists fit our expectations of those seeking proxy control.

A comparison of young and old Organizationalists on the attitudinal items reveals one remarkable difference: the young gave solid support to a policy of friendly relations with Cuba and with unspecified "Communist countries." As noted above, the Organi-

ιdy been found to be more leftist than Person-
∴ find the young going far beyond the position of
∠r Organizationalist. Such a result is all the more
ι one realizes that this leftward drift could at this time
ιction in Perón's own rhetoric.[21]

∠ 4.4 contains the position of each group on the summary
ιcal variate built from the attitudinal items which differen-
∟ ∠d the entire groups of Personalists and Organizationalists;
Figure 4.5 shows the major determinants of this attitudinal difference. It is important to note that in the case of the attitudinal
variate and each of its individual components, the young Peronists
are appreciably farther apart than are their older counterparts. The
positions of the two younger groups here reinforce the impression
given by the socioeconomic comparisons: if these two groups represented the future of Peronism, a deep schism in the movement
was assured.[22]

Only seven years later, the two Peronist factions actually did fall
into conflict with each other. Indeed, "fall into conflict" is too mild
a phrase: the two factions were quite literally at war, and substantial

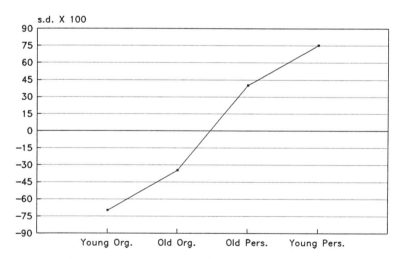

Figure 4.4 Age cohorts in charismatic dispersion: summary attitudinal
variate.

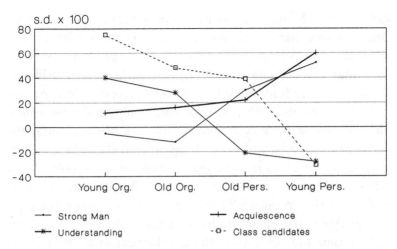

Figure 4.5 Age cohorts in charismatic dispersion: individual attitudinal factors.

loss of life occurred on both sides. The character of the warring camps is quite well predicted by the results presented here. This remarkable fit with subsequent events adds interest—and additional strength—to our findings.

Conclusions

The routinization of charisma is a process about which few well-grounded empirical statements can be made, especially in any detail. Of the two phases involved in the process, the first, which we have called the emergence of structure, seems more easily anticipated and understood, at least in broader terms. With the successful attraction of followers comes a progressively greater difficulty in maintaining coherence in the movement. Ultimately, it seems, the acceptance of institutionalized discipleship cannot be avoided if the leader's mission is not to founder; this is even more certain if the leader assumes the reins of government. The rate and degree of bureaucratization can depend upon a variety of circumstances, but one can be sure that with the development of a mass movement, the charismatic leader eventually must incorporate some intermediaries into structural locations that lie between the followers and the leader. This is a critical development, for with these intermediaries sooner or later must come dilution, erosion, and perhaps even deliberate distortion of the leader's mission as these secondary leaders, consciously or unconsciously, put their own stamp on the movement. Although the leader may employ a variety of means to delay this process, it cannot be withstood. Even in intensely ideological contexts, James March's succinct comment holds true: "People [that is, individuals] have goals; collectivities of people do not."[23] It is no small irony that in pursuit of these goals, the secondary figures, at least in this initial phase of charismatic routinization, invoke the leader's name and mission to legitimate their departures from orthodoxy. The charismatic leader faces two options: the movement can be institutionalized, thus facilitating the dispersion of charisma, or it can be resolutely unorganized, promoting confusion in, and ultimately the disintegration of, the mass following. Neither choice is likely to be acceptable.

There is a considerable body of organizational theory that speaks to the essential processes involved in the emergence of structure. However, with respect to the second phase of routinization—the dispersion of the mass charismatic response—there has been very little theoretical speculation and even less empirical investigation. The results presented in this chapter can be compared with no similar studies, and thus they must be offered as initial findings, awaiting discoveries from future research.

It seems that movement from a Personalist attachment to an Organization commitment (or, more likely, a commitment to secondary figures in the movement) is strongly dependent upon where the follower is located in the structure of society. More specifically, locations that facilitate awareness of, and *beneficial* contact with, the Organization apparatus and its personnel appear to be the locations where one finds a dispersion of charisma. Under such circumstances, attitudes that are important to the maintenance of the original charismatic bond are likely to erode. Absence from such locations seems to make it much more probable that those attitudes, and the charismatic bond itself, will remain intact.

What does the Peronist case teach us about the routinization of charisma? If we can say that the nature of the original Peronism was sure to change, that inevitably there would come greater differentiation within the movement, can we also say why the change took the shape it did? Was simple disintegration equally likely? Are there general lessons to be learned about the role of new recruits that can be drawn from our findings?

We believe our findings on the Personalists to be general. The main point is quite simple: many people in crisis are ready for, and some actively seek, proxy control. Once they have found a "savior" they do not readily let go. In Argentina, Personalists found in Juan Perón the answer to personal and collective crises. Organizationalists, having escaped those circumstances—or, in the case of the young Organizationalists, never having faced them—came to see Perón in a more dispassionate light. For them, charisma had dispersed and was gone.

If our interpretation is correct, it argues that all charismatic movements must founder in the face of success. This was precisely Weber's belief. When the crisis has passed, for whatever reason, the followers regain their sense of control and their sense of personal efficacy. The need for proxy control recedes. However, structural residue from the charismatic period may by that time have gained a bureaucratic life of its own. It is no surprise that even now, long after the death of Juan Perón, Peronism remains at the very center of Argentine politics.

The Residue of Charisma

When Juan Perón died on July 1, 1974, he was succeeded as president by his widow, María Estela Martínez de Perón (Isabel), whom he had insisted upon as his running mate in the elections of the preceding year. During the next two years political violence in Argentina accelerated at an astronomical rate. The conflict between Peronists on the left and right gave way to near random terror directed at and by self-styled revolutionaries on the one hand, and self-styled anticommunists on the other.

In the midst of this violence, the economy crumbled: inflation reached an annual rate exceeding 1000 percent and the nation was on the verge of bankruptcy. This plainly was an economic crisis, but unlike that of the early 1940s, it was not one which propelled large sectors of the public into psychological crisis. Although the enormous rate of inflation had dramatic effects, it was buffered in its impact by government wage policies, union contract settlements, and a social security program created by Perón. The specter of destitution did not emerge in public consciousness. There was indeed a crisis in the Argentina of 1976, and one with dramatic political implications, but it was not a crisis of widespread despair.

To the surprise of no one, in March of 1976 the armed forces replaced Isabel with a military junta. The third Peronist administration, of which so much had been expected, ended in total disaster.

The new military government set out to eliminate antiregime violence and to bring about economic recovery. The former goal was largely accomplished within three years, but at an extremely high price, as the government itself resorted to terrorist tactics.

Thousands of people were subjected to arbitrary arrest, imprison-ment, and torture; many simply disappeared. The nation's economic problems were much more difficult to resolve. Seven years of mil-itary rule left Argentina in even worse shape than it had been in 1976.

By 1982 the military government, welcomed six years earlier, was repudiated by most Argentines. This situation changed quite rap-idly, but also, as it turned out, quite briefly, on April 2, 1982, with the invasion of the Malvinas (Falkland Islands). The delight Argen-tines felt at the "recovery" of the islands was replaced by total disillusionment after the loss of the war with Great Britain. This ignominious defeat led almost immediately to the creation of a provisional government whose only purpose was the holding of elections to permit a return to constitutional rule.

On October 30, 1983, Argentines went to the polls for the first time in a decade, and to the amazement of most observers, chose as their new president a Radical, Raúl Alfonsín. For the first time ever, the Peronists lost a presidential election—and lost decisively. Their candidate, Italo Luder, received only 40 percent of the pop-ular vote; Alfonsín obtained 52 percent.

The only individual-level data available for analysis of the 1983 elections come from a survey by Darío Canton of five hundred voters in the Federal Capital (374) and the working-class suburb of La Matanza (126).[1] The sample is significantly flawed and cer-tainly cannot be assumed to well represent the overall electorate. It excluded females (for whom it was assumed that occupational data would not be readily available), which means that the level of support for Peronism is almost certainly exaggerated, since males, to a greater degree than females, tend to vote Peronist.[2] The inter-view completion rate was also quite low. Moreover, as was noted in Chapter 3, politically and economically, the Federal Capital dif-fers appreciably from the rest of the nation. For all these reasons, we are somewhat skeptical about these data as sources of reliable insights into the Peronism of 1983. Nevertheless, several findings are consistent with results from earlier analyses, as well as with the observations of journalists and others.

Peronist support among working-class voters in this sample was tepid, barely reaching majority status among unskilled workers and dropping far below that for skilled workers (see Table 5.1). Every other social group delivered resounding defeats to the Peronist candidate.

As historically has been the case, the Peronist vote in 1983 declined monotonically with increases in education. This time, however, the decline was quite dramatic; even among voters who had not finished primary school the Peronist candidate lost to his Radical opponent (35.2 percent to 44.1 percent).[3] Most interesting, in this study, about a fourth of the blue-collar workers who remembered voting Peronist in 1973 deserted the party ten years later (see Table 5.2). This was also true of a third of the self-employed, half the white-collar workers, and two-thirds of the members of liberal professions.[4] Overall, in this sample more than 40 percent of those who voted Peronist in 1973 failed to do so a decade later; remarkably, virtually all these deserters switched to the "enemy," the Radicals and Raúl Alfonsín.[5] In spite of the problems with such recall data, this percentage is impressive.

The same picture emerges when one examines the vote in sixteen socioeconomically homogeneous precincts in the Federal Capital.[6] Even in working-class areas—historically the strongholds of Peronism—Peronist candidates received only slightly more than a

Table 5.1 Presidential vote in the Federal Capital by occupation, 1983 (in percent).

Party	Unskilled Workers (N = 14)	Skilled Workers (N = 70)	Self-employed (N = 55)	White Collar (N =120)	Other (N = 115)
Peronist	50.0	42.9	25.4	15.8	9.6
Radical	35.7	37.1	54.5	60.8	73.0
Other	7.1	7.2	9.0	8.3	9.5
Unknown	7.1	12.9	10.9	15.0	7.8

Source: Darío Canton, El pueblo legislador: Las elecciones de 1983 (Buenos Aires: Centro Editor de América Latina, 1986), p. 48.

Table 5.2 1983 presidential vote by 1973 presidential vote in the Federal Capital (in percent).

	1973 Vote				
1983 vote	Peronist (N = 88)	Radical (N = 71)	Other (N = 40)	Didn't vote (N = 24)	Unknown (N = 39)
Peronist	59.1	1.4	10.0	8.3	0.0
Radical	37.5	97.2	57.5	50.0	38.5
Other	3.4	1.4	22.5	25.0	2.6
Unknown	0.0	0.0	10.0	16.7	59.0

Source: Darío Canton, *El pueblo legislador: Las elecciones de 1983* (Buenos Aires: Centro Editor de América Latina, 1986), p. 160.

third of the vote in 1983, down from 58 percent a decade earlier (see Figure 5.1). Looking across Figure 5.1, one can see that the decline in the Peronist vote was relatively uniform across class lines. The decline in working-class support is also evident in Figure 5.2. Note that in the Federal Capital Peronist candidates received a majority of the working-class vote only in 1946, 1951, and 1973, that is, in years when Perón himself was a presidential candidate.

In the 1973 presidential election, with Juan Perón at the top of the ticket, Peronism won as easily as it had two decades earlier. In 1983, without Juan Perón, Peronism lost rather ignominiously. Why?

We mentioned in Chapter 2 that Peronism was badly divided before its leader's death, and we showed in Chapter 4 that the roots of this division could be seen as early as 1965. There had never been a unifying Peronist ideology, nor had there been the need for one as long as Perón was alive.[7]

Perón had steadfastly refused to anoint a successor, or even a second in command.[8] One manifestation of his desire to retain control over his movement was that until 1973 Peronist candidates for major offices were selected by Perón himself. Peronism did have a formal party organization said to reach into each town, county, and province, but it was not a political party like the Radical or

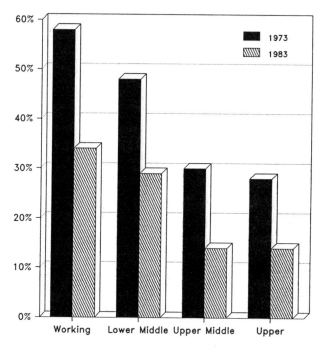

Figure 5.1 The Peronist vote in the Federal Capital by socioeconomic class, 1973 and 1983.

Conservative parties. Perón himself said that the Peronist Party functioned only for a few days prior to elections, and that as soon as the votes were counted it disappeared. Such a pattern was surely his intention, and he did his utmost to ensure that the structures in place did not usurp his influence. As we pointed out in Chapter 1, such an effort ultimately was futile. Structure emerges and gradually takes hold. In this case, however, Peronist party organizations competed with Peronist union organizations and Peronist government organizations. The party structure remained fragmented and weak—and Perón seemed more than content with this arrangement. Consequently, upon his death, Peronism had neither a unifying belief system, nor a coherent organizational structure, nor a leader.

In 1983 Peronism had to behave very much like the rest of the nation's political parties. For the first time there was some contro-

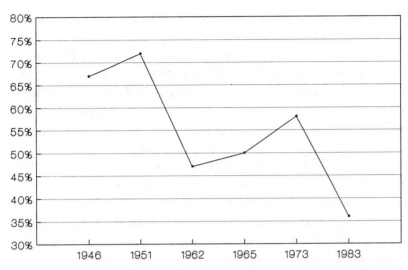

Figure 5.2 The Peronist vote in the Federal Capital, 1946–1983.

versy over the nomination of candidates. Since Perón had not named a successor, Peronism lacked an obvious presidential candidate. Italo Luder appears to have been selected largely because of his experience as acting president in 1975 while Isabel Perón was ill. An upper middle-class intellectual, Luder was completely lacking in the sort of personal appeal Peronists were accustomed to. That was especially evident in comparison with his dynamic Radical opponent, Raúl Alfonsín.

The Peronist candidate who seems most to have appealed to voter emotions was Herminio Iglesias, mayor of the archetypical working-class city of Avellaneda from 1973 to 1976, now aspiring to the governorship of the province of Buenos Aires, the second most powerful office in the Argentine political system. Iglesias, regularly accused of being a labor racketeer, based his campaign almost exclusively upon demagogy. At a Peronist rally in downtown Buenos Aires on the last day of the campaign, almost two million people watched in person and several million more on television as Iglesias burned a coffin draped with Radical colors. For many

Argentines Iglesias represented the violent past that they wanted desperately to forget.[9]

Carlos Grasso, a Peronist elected to the lower house of Congress from the Federal Capital, said of the party's campaign errors, "One of the major causes of our electoral losses was the fact that we kept considering societal aspirations that no longer correspond to reality."[10] This is an important point, for the Peronist campaign did seem to ignore the enormous changes that had taken place in Argentina since Perón's first election in 1946. For example, in 1947 only 18 percent of the residents of the Federal Capital owned their own homes; in 1980 that number was 68 percent.[11]

Emphasis upon the past instead of the present almost certainly was a mistake, but it may not have been uniformly disadvantageous. In Greater Buenos Aires the Peronists lost all the suburban counties abutting the Federal Capital, except La Matanza and the residential counties of San Isidro, San Fernando, Tigre, and Quilmes, but they won in the "second industrial belt," that is, those counties once removed from the capital, where there had been spectacular demographic growth between 1973 and 1983 as a consequence of continued migration from the interior. In 1983 Peronism fared best in those sections of Greater Buenos Aires that most closely resembled the areas of its greatest success in 1946: counties with the largest number of migrants. The product moment correlation between 1970–1980 demographic growth and the 1983 Peronist vote was +.771;[12] the correlation between demographic growth and the 1973–1983 change in the Peronist vote was +.949.[13]

After the 1983 election, divisions within Peronism seemed to multiply daily. One faction insisted that the electoral debacle was a result of not realizing that the movement still had a single leader—María Estela Martínez de Perón. However, Isabel had returned to Spain and appeared uninterested in the internecine conflicts within the movement her husband had founded. The trade union movement, still overwhelmingly Peronist, at least in principle, was as badly divided as the political sector. And though no longer a major force, there remained an extreme left within Peronism. Former Montoneros, now calling themselves Revolutionary Peronism, again became an organized faction within the Peronist Party (now actually the Partido Justicialista). Divisions within Peronism were epitomized by the fact that in 1987 the twenty Peronist senators were divided into eight formal blocs, four of which had a single member.

Shortly after the 1983 electoral defeat a group of moderate Peronist politicians, calling themselves Renovators, set out to convert Peronism into a modern political party, democratically organized, with a definite program. In the congressional elections of 1985 their candidates competed with other Peronist candidates in several parts of the country. In the province of Buenos Aires the Renovating slate of candidates overwhelmed the Orthodox slate loyal to Iglesias by a margin of almost a three to one. Iglesias was unable to carry even his own voting booth (*mesa*).

In these elections the Peronists lost seven seats in the Chamber of Deputies as their share of the popular vote dropped under 36 percent.[14] The results greatly improved the position of the Renovators and allowed one of their leaders, Antonio Cafiero, to gain control of the party in the all-important province of Buenos Aires. Two years later, in the far more important gubernatorial elections, an at least partially "renovated" Peronism gained control of a majority of the nation's provinces. Antonio Cafiero was elected governor of Buenos Aires, giving him a great advantage over his competitors for the presidential nomination in 1989.

Union leaders, who dominated the Peronist movement after 1955, saw in the Renovators a threat to their continued domination. In the congressional debate of a new union organization bill that President Alfonsín claimed would lead to greater union democracy, one Peronist deputy, himself a union leader, said, "if the union movement is split Peronism is also split. . . . The political movement rests upon us; we are its backbone."[15]

The most important of the Renovators' renovations was the establishment of a national party primary for the selection of presidential candidates. In spite of his control of the party apparatus and the support of most Peronist governors, Cafiero's nomination was challenged by Carlos Saúl Menem, *caudillo* of the poor province of La Rioja. Cafiero offered Peronists a relatively clear program; Menem simply promised a return to the glorious days of yesteryear. Menem also played on the anti-*porteño* sentiment still strong in the poorer provinces of the interior (*porteños* are the residents of the city of Buenos Aires).

On July 9, 1988, Peronist rank and file had a voice for the first time in the selection of their presidential candidate. Menem received 53 percent of the vote. He rolled up huge majorities in the poorer western provinces,[16] and in the poorer counties surrounding the Federal Capital, while losing to Cafiero in the more developed areas of the country. Less than half of the four million Peronist party members cast a ballot.

With Alfonsín ineligible for reelection, the Radicals chose the governor of Córdoba, Eduardo Angeloz, as their candidate. In retrospect, it appears that Angeloz never had a chance. He was saddled with the economic disaster of the preceding six years.[17] Menem offered few specific programs, but he repeated over and over again, "Follow me!" Almost half the voters did so, and Menem received 47 percent of the popular vote to Angeloz' 37 percent.[18]

After Peronism's resounding electoral defeats in 1983 and 1985 one might have suspected that the party might not long outlive its founder. However, given the fact that Peronism in 1990 had a majority of the seats in both houses of Congress and control of a majority of the provinces, in addition to the presidency, it seems more likely that this once charismatic movement has now become fully institutionalized. As President Menem himself put it, "Peronism of today is not the Peronism of 1946, nor even the Peronism of the 1973–1976 period."[19]

On the Formation of a Charismatic Bond

The charismatic bond is a product of circumstance. The would-be leader must at the right moment provide for his audience, through a combination of personal attributes and seemingly effective actions, a basis for adoration. Those same attributes and actions at any other time, though they might be useful and admired, would not strike the necessary chord of response. The right moment comes when the incipient followers, feeling rather abruptly unable to cope with their fundamental problems, are ready—and indeed anxious—to assign responsibility for solving these problems to a reliable proxy. From hopelessness and despair the followers move to joy and relief, as the charismatic bond is forged.

Psychological crisis, then, is essential to the emergence of charisma. Moreover, such a crisis probably must be relatively abrupt. A more prolonged crisis would have the effect of wholly undermining self-efficacy—not even through a proxy could control be regained —and, would do so in a context in which the environment seemed irreversibly negative. The response in that situation, self-efficacy theory argues, would be despondency and withdrawal.

In the case of political charisma, the triggering crisis must be large-scale rather than individual. Individual crises are always present in a population. Serious illnesses, economic reversals, failures in intimate social ties are scattered continuously through all societies. They may well precipitate breakdowns in self-efficacy for those involved, but such individualized crises normally do not get aggregated into collective need. For macroscopic need to develop, large numbers of people must *simultaneously* come to feel they no longer can cope. This is an occurrence which invariably is tied to events of great and sweeping magnitude, such as war, revolution, famine, or economic collapse.[20]

In this case, economic collapse, specifically the collapse of the agricultural sector in Argentina, triggered mass migration to cities. This migration overwhelmed urban social and economic structures, populated the *villas miserias,* left huge numbers living at the very margin of existence, and kept urban wage rates at depression levels, even for those not coming from the countryside.

Not *all* societal disruptions or economic reversals will result in mass readiness for charismatic bonding. One should not expect self-efficacy feelings to be easily undermined. Positive feelings of efficacy must often be tied, psychologically, to a more generalized sense of personal significance, a belief that one counts in this world. Intuitively, one would expect such a sentiment to be both valued and defended by its holder, in which case the evidence accepted by that holder as fully confirming could be of a weaker character—vicarious experience or verbal persuasion, in Bandura's terms, rather than actual performance attainments. The other side of this coin is that evidence persuasive of a failure in one's own coping capacity must be striking indeed. Performance failures, which are often of ambiguous cause, will whenever possible be blamed upon environmental circumstance.[21]

Normal economic swings or mild social disorders are not the stuff of psychological crisis, though they may cast some doubt in the minds of citizens about their own control over events.[22] In any event, catastrophes of sufficient scope and magnitude inevitably do come and are even recurrent. For Weber, of course, these were the foundation of recurrent charisma, though whether such catastrophes should be seen as cycles in a larger Weberian theory of history is open to question.

What happens with lesser social or economic reversals—when events, if not truly frightening, are at least worrisome, and when self-efficacy, if not in eclipse, is at least challenged? Might devotion to a charismatic proxy be only the extreme form of a general disposition to favor centralized influence structures when a population confronts a problematic and stressful environment? In other words, is the collective response leading to charismatic bonding different in kind or only in degree? As noted in Chapter 1, there is a good deal of social psychological evidence that under stressful conditions, people gravitate toward centralized influence structures. There also is the "rally round the flag" effect found in U.S. public opinion data in times of international tension—times, presumably, when the citizenry feels somewhat less able to understand and control events. More directly pertinent is the U.S. survey evidence showing a greater preference for "strong leaders" among those who feel politically inefficacious. And from several countries come data correlating high political self-efficacy with support for democratic (that is, dispersed influence) arrangements.[23] These findings all suggest the possibility that charismatic bonding is indeed the extreme manifestation of a general disposition toward centralized and (necessarily) personalized authority in times of stress —and toward its opposite in times when collective self-efficacy is flourishing. Much better evidence is needed here, of course. If the general point is correct, however, we may anticipate swings in autocratic/democratic proclivities in mass publics as stressful circumstances come and go. This would be true even in the absence of any occurrences of charismatic bonding, which would require more than mere stress to be triggered.

In this study we lack systematic evidence regarding what proof an incipient following must see in order to bond with a leader, and what proof an existing following must see in order to sustain the charismatic bond. These are important questions. Psychological readiness for a savior plainly does not lead a public to seize upon the first available candidate for that role. Something—very probably a mixture of style and substance, of promise and performance— must be seen in the would-be leader which persuades the public that this is the one to turn to. Moreover, if this figure is, by proxy, to sustain the sense of self-efficacy in the following, he or she must appear to be in some sense the *agent* of that following. Mass belief in such agency, too, will play into the choice of a leader in the first place, though the evidence of agency may be entirely rhetorical.

We pointed out in Chapter 2 that the evidence which Perón presented to his incipient following came out of actions he undertook while minister of labor. This evidence was a blend of concrete policies, which addressed the severe economic problems of the urban workers, and symbolic appeals, which addressed their equally severe psychic wounds. We cannot say what the mix was in the minds of the beholders, nor can we assess the importance of each element and how that importance may have changed as Peronism emerged. Our data are not adequate for such specification. It does seem, however, that both concrete and symbolic factors must have contributed to the view that Perón was indeed the agent of his followers. On the one hand, he did their bidding in making wage policy; on the other hand, he said directly and repeatedly that he was one of them, that he was like them, that he supported them.

What sort of performance is needed to sustain and perhaps even enhance mass commitment to a savior? Obviously, we cannot with a single case specify a theoretical answer to that question, but it is clear that in the case at hand the performance was dramatic. The average real wage in Argentina took off in 1945, and by 1949 it was almost 75 percent above the 1945 level.[24] Although real wages then declined from that high, at the time of Perón's exile the average remained more than 50 percent above the 1945 figure. Equally important, between 1946 and 1955 the Peronist government implemented social security and employment security reforms which for the most vulnerable elements of Argentine society largely ended the most frightening aspects of economic recession. It is little wonder that Perón was adored by his beneficiaries (and hated by those who saw themselves as paying the costs of the social programs). Still, it remains an open question how long this adoration would have continued had he stayed in power and himself confronted the storms on the economic horizon. In this regard, exile may have been the ideal vehicle for sustaining a bond with his public.

In spite of the evidence from the Perón case, we cannot assume that such dramatic results are necessary to sustain the charismatic bond. Once the following feels both devotion and dependence, it cannot be expected to see events entirely clearly. We know that in small groups leaders have more freedom than followers to wander from group norms without sacrificing status, and that leaders' performances are seen by those of lesser status as more successful than is warranted by the facts.[25] Hence, it does not seem far-fetched to argue that, at least in the short run, ambivalent data on a charismatic leader's performance may well be interpreted by a following in wholly positive terms. The case of Franklin Delano Roosevelt is illustrative. Roosevelt was a leader who personalized the response of government to economic crisis, who represented a coalition of disparate interests supporting change, who inspired ardent support from a mass public, but who in his first term was anything but heroic in actual accomplishments, and who in point of fact was considerably less different from his despised predecessor than the public (or most scholars) realized.[26] Nonetheless, his extraordinary standing in the mass public does not appear to have suffered. It was as if Roosevelt could not fail in the eyes of his public, except perhaps under circumstances in which failure was both stark and dramatic. We cannot know over what time span a very popular leader may hang on while delivering marginal results. No doubt the intensity of the crisis involved is a crucial factor.

On the Evolution of a Charismatic Bond

Questions about sustaining a charismatic bond can be subsumed under a general discussion of the evolution of that bond. In Chapter 1 we discussed that evolution in terms of two processes. First comes the emergence of structure as the charismatic movement becomes rooted in the larger society and, possibly, in its government. Later comes the dispersion of the charismatic response, as secondary leaders become important and relatively independent sources of benefits—material and perhaps psychological as well—for elements of the following.

What happens to the self-efficacy of the mass of followers during this evolution? Our speculation, given some support by the data presented in Chapter 4, is that those followers who reach the second stage of the process experience a considerable loss of emotional fervor. Their commitment, now to the movement and its lesser figures rather than to the savior, has evolved into a form rather like partisan identification—that is, more a standing commitment of general support than a passionate linking of one's life and fortunes to the leader. This is not to say that the commitment has lost all of its punch; like partisan identification, it can still be crucial to decisions about political action. But lacking the direct and powerful self-efficacy implications, it necessarily must lose some steam.

Thus we would not expect *any* charismatic bond to have staying power over more than a few generations. If the leader demonstrably fails to ameliorate conditions of his following, the bond will fail— though perhaps only gradually, because some will be more willing to see failure than others. If the leader and the movement succeed, the restored sense of efficacy among the followers will undermine the passion of their commitment. Of course, success will not be complete; some followers will lie beyond its reach and, paradoxically, therefore will be more likely, absent clear evidence of hopelessness, to retain commitment to the personalist savior. Still, even for such elements, it will probably become progressively more difficult to pass their passionate conviction on to offspring.

Many questions remain. For example, what will be the response of an incipient following if the leader is prematurely removed from the scene? How would the politicization of the urban workers have changed had Perón been killed by his jailers in 1945 and the charismatic bond never formed? If Perón had died in his first term, would his political legacy have died with him? It might be argued that there was no understudy waiting in the wings, no apprentice with the record and the reputation needed to be elevated to the status of savior. But what about Eva? She was central to Perón's success and was the object of considerable esteem, if not reverence. It is a fascinating question whether, if so disposed, she could have assumed the mantle of charisma. Our general presumption is that a charismatic movement is fragile in that it is highly particularistic; normally it cannot survive the early death of the leader. But what path distintegration would follow cannot be surmised. Exile or imprisonment of the leader may be an entirely different matter; the bond conceivably could be sustained for some time on the basis of hope.

After a charismatic leader is fully rooted in a society, his or her political legacy would seem assured. First, the politics of the society is very likely to have been reoriented around the leader and the movement; even after the leader's departure from the scene, political contests and debates will probably revolve around his or her initiatives and undertakings, both real and mythical. Second, and perhaps more important in the long run, there will be a bureaucratic residue from the leader's time in power. The structures and organizations put in place by the movement-cum-government are unlikely to be dislodged, short of a systemic collapse, even though the leader is no longer in place. A large body of literature gives testimony to the staying power of bureaucracies in a variety of regimes and under variable conditions. There is no reason to suppose that a post-charisma regime would be different.

Finally, what happens if in the midst of macroscopic crisis no leader appears? Could this actually happen—or would those needing a savior ultimately find one plausible enough to anoint? If so, how far would they reach? How much evidence of leadership would be sought? Would choices end up being fragmented and localized rather than coherent and centralized? Our argument is that the affected mass public is primed, that it is ready for a magnetic leader. Unfortunately, we cannot go beyond that; we cannot answer these questions. It does seem, however, that ideology alone will never fill the void. We can think of no historical example in which, when masses of people cried out for salvation, ideas alone won them over. Even in the Marxist case, this point is made: "According to the official claims of the ideology, all objectives are collective and the decisions taken to achieve them are taken collectively. Yet charisma and the attendant cult of personality have played a major part in the evolution of communist systems. . . . During the heroic phase of the revolution a dominant figure appears to be necessary."[27] For the masses, then, ideology may follow, but a Lenin must lead.

Juan Perón and his movement were the central features of Argentine political life for more than forty years. Perón was considered by large numbers of Argentine voters to be more than their leader; he was their saint. And yet the truth is that though Perón did improve the lot of the working classes, his leadership was not an unmixed blessing, even for them. His social and economic policies set off virulent inflation and poisoned relations between social strata. Out of his regime emerged an Argentina which fell progressively further behind the set of Western nations with which its living standard had for thirty years been compared. Indeed, Argentina fell to near Third World status.

Nevertheless, for those who loved him, these problems were beside the point. In an interview with one of the authors during Perón's exile years, a lower-level labor leader, Peronist to the core, was asked why he remained devoted to this particular savior. After all, it was pointed out to him, Perón's policies in the end had not greatly improved his material existence. It makes no difference, was his answer. "Before Perón I was poor and I was nobody; now I am only poor."

**Notes
Bibliography
Index**

Notes

1. On the Appearance and Evolution of Charisma

1. Dean Keith Simonton, *Genius, Creativity, and Leadership: Historiometric Inquiries* (Cambridge: Harvard University Press, 1984), p. 121.

2. A. M. Henderson and Talcott Parsons, eds., *The Theory of Social and Economic Organization* (New York: Oxford University Press, 1947), pp. 358–359.

3. Max Weber, *Economy and Society* (New York: Bedminster Press, 1968).

4. Of course, there are exceptions. Franz Neumann, in discussing anxiety and politics, argued that fear and "a nearly total ego-shrinkage" are what push masses into readiness for "caesaristic" leadership. See *The Democratic and Authoritarian State* (New York: Free Press, 1957), pp. 270–295. Irvine Schiffer, in his book *Charisma: A Psychoanalytic Look at Mass Society* (Toronto: University of Toronto Press, 1973), is even more explicit, arguing that charismatic leaders appear when the call comes from a rescue-hungry people. And James C. Davies presents some data to support a similar argument in his "Charisma in the 1952 Campaign," *The American Political Science Review* 48 (1954), 1083–1102.

5. Alvin W. Gouldner, "Introduction," in Gouldner, ed., *Studies in Leadership* (New York: Harper and Brothers, 1950), pp. 21–31.

6. Cecil A. Gibb, "Leadership," in Gardner Lindzay and Elliot Aronson, eds., *Handbook of Social Psychology*, vol. 1 (Reading, Mass.: Addison-Wesley, 1969), pp. 568–614.

7. Harold Lasswell, *Power and Personality* (New York: Viking Press, 1948), p. 10.

8. Robert A. Dahl, "Power," in David L. Sills, ed., *International Encyclopedia of the Social Sciences*, vol. 12 (New York: Free Press, 1968), pp. 405–415; Dahl, *Modern Political Analysis*, 4th ed. (Englewood Cliffs, N.J.: Prentice-Hall, 1984).

9. Ann Ruth Wilner, *The Spellbinders: Charismatic Political Leadership* (New Haven: Yale University Press, 1984).

10. José Enrique Miguens, "The Presidential Elections of 1973 and the End of Ideology," in Frederick C. Turner and José Enrique Miguens, eds., *Juan Perón and the Reshaping of Argentina* (Pittsburgh: Pittsburgh University Press, 1983), pp. 150–152.

11. Sidney G. Winter, Jr., "Concepts of Rationality in Behavioral Theory," University of Michigan, Institute of Public Policy Studies, Discussion Paper no. 7, 1969.

12. Ibid., p. 26.

13. R. B. Zajonc, "Feeling and Thinking: Preferences Need No Inferences," *American Psychologist* 35 (1980), 151–175.

14. Theodore Abel's work on Nazi followers, *The Nazi Movement* (New York: Atherton, 1965), is something of an exception, although its methodology leaves much to be desired. The usual work on Nazis has involved more assumptions about national character or psychopathology assumptions than empirical study.

15. Albert Bandura, "Self-Efficacy: Toward a Unifying Theory of Behavioral Change," *Psychological Review* 84 (1977), 191–215; Bandura, "Self-Efficacy Mechanism in Human Agency," *American Psychologist* 37 (1982), 122–147; Bandura, *Social Foundations of Thought and Action* (Englewood Cliffs, N.J.: Prentice-Hall, 1986).

16. See Richard Nisbett and Lee Ross, *Human Inference: Strategies and Shortcomings of Social Judgment* (Englewood Cliffs, N.J.: Prentice-Hall, 1980).

17. Douglas Madsen, "Political Self-Efficacy Tested," *American Political Science Review* 81 (1987), 571–581; Patricia Gurin and Orville G. Brim, Jr., "Change in Self in Adulthood: The Example of Sense of Control," *Life-Span Development and Behavior* 6 (1984), 282–334.

18. Note that this scenario presupposes change which does not occur so slowly as to be very difficult to perceive—as could well be the case were it to occur over many generations.

19. Suzanne M. Miller, "Predictability and Human Stress: Towards a Clarification of Evidence and Theory," in Leonard Berkowitz, ed., *Advances in Experimental Social Psychology*, vol. 14 (New York: Academic Press, 1981), pp. 203–256.

20. Bandura, "Self-Efficacy Mechanism," p. 142.

21. Much more empirical work on the particulars of both proxy selection and its consequences is needed. The work by psychologists on impression formation offers useful guidance, however, especially with respect to unification and integration of perceptions of a leader by the mass public. For a useful review of this work, see Roger Brown, *Social Psychology: The Second Edition* (New York: Free Press, 1985), chap. 11.

22. A voluminous clinical literature treats aspects of human bonding, with special reference to how in very early life bonding, or its absence, plays into personality disorders which appear later on. This work is grounded largely in ego psychology, but some relatively recent examples—notably, the work of Bowlby on attachment theory—are tied to ethology. Often therapeutic in nature, this clinical literature emerges from research directed at identifying and understanding the deepest psychological roots of the human propensity for attachment. Such a goal goes well beyond our present purpose, although there surely are points of theoretical overlap between that research and our own. See Schiffer, *Charisma*; Zanvel A. Liff, *The Leader in the Group* (New York: Jason Aronson, 1975); W. R. Bion, *Attention and Interpretation* (London: Tavistock, 1970); and Victoria Hamilton, "Some Problems in the Clinical Application of Attachment Theory," *Psychoanalytic Psychotherapy* 3 (1987), 67–83.

23. Robert E. Lane, *Political Ideology* (New York: Free Press, 1962), p. 75.

24. Arthur Koestler, "The Initiates," in Richard Crossman, ed., *The God That Failed* (New York: Harper, 1949), pp. 17–23.

25. Hadley Cantril, *The Politics of Despair* (New York: Collier, 1958), pp. 86–94.

26. Roland L. Warren, "German *Partilieder* and Christian Hymns as Instruments of Social Control," *Journal of Abnormal Social Psychology* 38 (1943), 96–100.

27. Christopher Edwards, *Crazy for God* (Englewood Cliffs, N.J.: Prentice-Hall, 1979), pp. 14–16, 107, 191.

28. Abel, *The Nazi Movement*.

29. Peter H. Merkl, *Political Violence under the Swastika: 581 Early Nazis* (Princeton, N.J.: Princeton University Press, 1975); Merkl, *The Making of a Storm Trooper* (Princeton, N.J.: Princeton University Press, 1980).

30. Merkl, *The Making*, pp. 114–115.

31. Ibid., p. 205.

32. Morris Janowitz and Dwaine Marvick, "Authoritarianism and Political Behavior," *Public Opinion Quarterly* 17 (1953), 185–201.

33. Muzafer Sherif et al., *Intergroup Conflict and Cooperation: The Robber's Cave Experiment* (Norman, Okla.: University Book Exchange, 1960).

34. Robert Blake and Jane Mouton, "Reactions to Intergroup Competition under Win-Lose Conditions," *Management Science* 7 (1961), 420–435.

35. For data on some particulars of that reaction, see John Archer, *Animals under Stress* (Baltimore: University Park Press, 1979).

36. J. T. Lanzetta, "Group Behavior under Stress," *Human Relations* 8 (1955), 29–52.

37. Samuel Stouffer et al., *The American Soldier* (Princeton, N.J.: Princeton University Press, 1949); Edward A. Shils and Morris Janowitz, "Cohesion and

Disintegration in the *Wehrmacht* in World War II," *Public Opinion Quarterly* 12 (1948), 280–315.

38. Avner Ziv, Arie W. Kruglansky, and Shmuel Shulman, "Children's Psychological Reactions to Wartime Stress," *Journal of Personality and Social Psychology* 30 (1974), 24–30.

39. D. J. W. Strümpfer, "Fear and Anxiety during a Disaster," *Journal of Social Psychology* 82 (1970), 263–268; Martha Wolfenstein, *Disaster* (Glencoe, Ill.: Free Press, 1957).

40. Irving L. Janis, *Victims of Groupthink* (Boston: Houghton Mifflin, 1972).

41. Stanley Schachter, *The Psychology of Affiliation* (Stanford: Stanford University Press, 1959).

42. H. H. Kelley et al., "Collective Behavior in a Simulated Panic Situation," *Journal of Experimental Social Psychology* 1 (1965), 20–54.

43. R. L. Helmreich and B. E. Collins, "Situational Determinants of Affiliative Preferences under Stress," *Journal of Personality and Social Psychology* 6 (1957), 79–85.

44. John Renner and Vivian Renner, "Effects of Stress on Group versus Individual Problem Solving," *Psychological Reports* 30 (1972), 487–491.

45. Leonard L. Rosenbaum and William B. Rosenbaum, "Moral and Productivity Consequences of Group Leadership Style, Stress, and Type of Task," *Journal of Applied Psychology* 55 (1971), 343–348.

46. Robert Hamblin, "Group Integration during a Crisis," *Human Relations* 11 (1958), 67–76; Hamblin, "Leadership and Crises," *Sociometry* 21 (1958), 322–335.

47. See Arthur H. Miller et al., "Schematic Assessments of Presidential Candidates," *American Political Science Review* 80 (1986), 521–540; Donald R. Kinder, "Presidential Prototypes," *Political Behavior* 2 (1982), 315–337; and Douglas Madsen, "Political Information Processing in an Electoral Context," *International Political Science Review* 2 (1981), 423–443.

48. Nisbet and Ross, *Human Inference,* chap. 3.

49. This will surprise no one who has observed fans' attributions of general expertise and wisdom to various stars in the entertainment world. But see Sherif et al., *Intergroup Conflict,* for clear and systematic evidence on this point.

50. Brown, *Social Psychology,* pp. 424–426.

51. Howard Schuman and Jacqueline Scott, "Generations and Collective Memories," *American Sociological Review* 54 (1989), 359–381; Paul Allen Beck, "A Socialization Theory of Partisan Realignment," in Richard Niemi and Herbert Weisberg, eds., *Controversies in American Voting Behavior* (San Francisco: W. H. Freeman, 1976), pp. 396–411; M. Kent Jennings, "Residues of a Movement: The Aging of the American Protest Generation," *American Political Science Review* 81 (1987), 367–382.

52. See especially Herbert A. Simon, *Administrative Behavior* (New York:

Free Press, 1976); and Richard M. Cyert and Kenneth R. MacCrimmon, "Organizations," in Gardner Lindzay and Elliot Aronson, eds., *Handbook of Social Psychology*, vol. 1 (Reading, Mass.: Addison-Wesley, 1969), pp. 568–614.

53. On social identification generally, see Michael A. Hogg and Dominic Abrams, *Social Identifications* (New York: Routledge, 1988); and Brown, *Social Psychology*. On political identification, see the introduction by S. M. Lipset and Stein Rokkan in their edited volume *Party Systems and Voter Alignments* (New York: Free Press, 1967); and the works cited in note 51.

54. See the references in notes 33, 34, 36 and 37.

55. See Brown, *Social Psychology*, chap. 6.

56. Henri Tajfel, *Human Groups and Social Categories* (Cambridge: Cambridge University Press, 1981); Henri Tajfel and J. C. Turner, "An Intregrative Theory of Social Conflict," in W. Austin and S. Worchel, eds., *The Social Psychology of Intergroup Relations* (Monterey, Calif.: Brooks/Cole, 1979) pp. 33–47; Hogg and Abrams, *Social Identifications*.

57. Edward Shils, "The Concentration and Dispersion of Charisma: Their Bearing on Economic Policy in Underdeveloped Countries," *World Politics* 11 (1958), 1–19.

58. Cyert and MacCrimmon, "Organizations," p. 585.

59. Dwaine Marvick, "Party Cadres and Receptive Party Voters in the 1967 Indian National Election," *Asian Survey* 10 (1970), 953.

60. Hugh Heclo, "Introduction: The Presidential Illusion," in Hugh Heclo and Lester M. Salaman, eds., *The Illusion of Presidential Government* (Boulder: Westview Press, 1981), p. 1.

61. Edward Shils, "Charisma, Order, and Status," *American Sociological Review* 30 (1965), 206. Emphasis added.

2. Peronism: Its Context and Evolution

1. Julio Oyhanarte, "Historia del poder judicial," *Todo es Historia* 6 (1972), 92.

2. A. G. Ford, "British Investment and Argentine Economic Development, 1880–1914," in David Rock, ed., *Argentina in the Twentieth Century* (Pittsburgh: University of Pittsburgh Press, 1975), p. 14.

3. Juan E. Corradi, *The Fitful Republic: Economy, Society, and Politics in Argentina* (Boulder: Westview Press, 1985), p. 30.

4. Dirección Nacional de Estadística y Censos, *Segundo censo de la República Argentina* (Buenos Aires: n.p., 1898), vol. II, p. clxxvii, vol. III, pp. clxii, clxiv.

5. David Rock, *Politics in Argentina, 1890–1930: The Rise and Fall of Radicalism* (London: Cambridge University Press, 1975), p. 11.

6. Oscar Cornblit, "Inmigrantes y empresarios en la política argentina," in

Torcuato DiTella and Tulio Halperín Donghi, eds., *Los fragmentos del poder* (Buenos Aires: Editorial Jorge Alvarez, 1969), p. 416.

7. Ysabel Rennie, *The Argentine Republic* (New York: Macmillan, 1945), p. 166.

8. Carlos H. Waisman, *Reversal of Development in Argentina: Postwar Counterrevolutionary Politics and Their Structural Consequences* (Princeton, N.J.: Princeton University Press, 1987), pp. 78–82.

9. For greater detail on this first Radical administration, see Peter G. Snow, *Argentine Radicalism: The History and Doctrine of the Radical Civic Union* (Iowa City: University of Iowa Press, 1965).

10. José Luis Romero, *A History of Argentine Political Thought* (Stanford: Stanford University Press, 1963), pp. 234–241; Rodolfo Puiggrós, *La democracia fraudulenta* (Buenos Aires: Editorial Jorge Alvarez, 1968).

11. Richard Walter, *The Socialist Party of Argentina, 1890–1930* (Austin: University of Texas Press, 1977), p. 125.

12. Gino Germani, "El surgimiento del Peronismo: El rol de los obreros y de los migrantes internos," *Desarrollo Económico* 13 (1973), 479.

13. Cited in Carlos Díaz Alejandro, *Essays on the Economic History of the Argentine Republic* (New Haven: Yale University Press, 1970), p. 108.

14. Germani, "El surgimiento," p. 452.

15. Roberto Carri, *Sindicatos y poder en la Argentina* (Buenos Aires: Editorial Sudestada, 1967), p. 27.

16. Shortly after he became its head, the Labor Secretariat was raised to cabinet status.

17. Austin F. MacDonald, *Latin American Politics and Government* (New York: Thomas Y. Crowell, 1954), p. 79.

18. Ruth Greenup and Leonard Greenup, *Revolution before Breakfast* (Chapel Hill: University of North Carolina Press, 1945), p. 167.

19. Díaz Alejandro, *Essays*, pp. 124, 430.

20. Germani, "El surgimiento," pp. 450–452.

21. Hugo E. Ratier, *Villeros y villas miserias* (Buenos Aires: Centro Editor de América Latina, 1971), pp. 13–14.

22. David Tamarin, *The Argentine Labor Movement, 1930–1945: A Study in the Origins of Peronism* (Albuquerque: University of New Mexico Press, 1985), p. 198.

23. Germani, "El surgimiento," p. 479.

24. See Joseph Page, *Perón: A Biography* (New York: Random House, 1983), p. 132; Tad Szulc, *Twilight of the Tyrants* (New York: Henry Holt, 1959), p. 123; Félix Luna, *El 45* (Buenos Aires: Editorial Jorge Alvarez, 1969), pp. 342–378; and Félix Luna, *Argentina de Perón a Lanusse* (Barcelona: Editorial Planeta, 1972), pp. 30–31.

25. *The Times* (London), October 19, 1945, p. 4.

26. Luna, *Argentina,* pp. 30–31. Emphasis added. See also Paul H. Lewis, *The Crisis of Argentine Capitalism* (Chapel Hill: University of North Carolina Press, 1990), p. 143, where this is even described as "an almost mystical dialogue between leader and mass. It was a spectacle of charisma's power."

27. Luna, *El 45,* p. 371.

28. Ibid., p. 375.

29. Greenup and Greenup, *Revolution,* p. 162.

30. Page, *Perón,* p. 148.

31. Daniel James, *Resistance and Integration: Peronism and the Argentine Working Class, 1946–1976* (New York: Cambridge University Press, 1988), p. 10, reports that during Perón's first term as president, union membership increased from 520,000 to 2,334,000. See also Benjamin A. Most, "Authoritarianism and the Growth of the State: An Assessment of Their Impact on Argentine Public Policy, 1930–1970," *Comparative Political Studies* 13 (1980), 180; and Juan Carlos d'Abate, "Trade Unions and Peronism," in Frederick C. Turner and José Enrique Miguens, eds., *Juan Perón and the Reshaping of Argentina* (Pittsburgh: Pittsburgh University Press, 1983), p. 57.

32. Gary Wynia, *Argentina in the Postwar Era: Politics and Economic Policy Making in a Divided Society* (Albuquerque: University of New Mexico Press, 1968), p. 62, says that salary income as a percentage of national income increased from 38.7 percent in 1946 to 45.7 percent in 1949. Corradi, *The Fitful Republic,* p. 64, says that labor's share of national income increased from 45 percent in 1943 to 59 percent in 1949.

33. Díaz Alejandro, *Essays,* p. 429.

34. Ratier, *Villeros,* p. 26.

35. Daniel James, "The Peronist Left, 1955–1975," *Journal of Latin American Studies* 8 (1976), 294.

36. For a discussion of sex-based differences in Argentine voting behavior see Peter G. Snow, *Political Forces in Argentina* (New York: Praeger Special Editions, 1979), pp. 40–41.

37. Eva Perón, *My Mission in Life* (New York: Vantage Press, 1953), p. iii.

38. The best English-language biography of Evita is probably Nicolas Fraser and Marysa Navarro, *Eva Perón* (New York: W. W. Norton, 1980). An excellent study of the myths surrounding her life is J. M. Taylor, *Eva Perón: The Myths of a Woman* (Chicago: University of Chicago Press, 1979).

39. Gary W. Wynia, *Argentina: Illusions and Realities* (New York: Holmes and Meier, 1986), p. 60.

40. Marvin Goldwert, "Dichotomies of Militarism in Argentina," *Orbis* 10 (1966), 933.

41. Frondizi has always denied the existence of such a deal with Perón; in a personal interview with one of the authors in 1967 he said "there was no pact whatsoever." For a published denial see Félix Luna, *Diálogos con Frondizi*

(Buenos Aires: Editorial Desarrollo, 1963), p. 40. Perón insisted with equal vigor, however, that a deal was made and that Frondizi refused to live up to it. In a 1965 letter to one of the authors Perón said the agreement was that described in Ricardo C. Guardo, *Horas difíciles* (Buenos Aires: Ediciones Ricardo C. Guardo, 1963), pp. 109–111. It is probably not very important whether or not a formal deal was made; what is important is that most Argentines, and virtually all military leaders, believed that the deal had been made, and acted accordingly.

42. Carri, *Sindicatos,* p. 119.

43. The electoral reform of 1911 established compulsory male suffrage, and when women were enfranchised in 1947, they too were required to vote. Casting a blank ballot allowed voters to comply with the law and at the same time register their displeasure with the electoral process. In 1957 and 1960 more ballots were left blank than were cast for any single party. Virtually all these blank ballots were cast by Peronists obeying the wishes of their leader.

44. Ramón Andino and Eduardo J. Paredes, *Breve historia de los partidos políticos argentinos* (Buenos Aires: Alzamor Editores, 1974), p. 173.

45. Ministerio del Interior, Departamento Electoral, "Elección de diputados nacionales, 14-III-1965: Resultados por distrito" (mimeo).

46. For the last thirty years it has been illegal to use the name of an individual in the name of a political party. Justicialism, the name given by Perón to his ersatz political philosophy, is the title most often used by the Peronists for their political party.

47. Richard Gillespie, *Soldiers of Perón: Argentina's Montoneros* (London: Oxford University Press, 1982), pp. 178–179.

48. Ibid., pp. 54–60.

49. James, "Peronist Left," p. 284.

50. Gillespie, *Soldiers,* pp. 131–132.

51. Although the Montoneros were the largest guerrilla group, there were several others, most notably the Trotskyite People's Revolutionary Army (ERP).

52. Gillespie, *Soldiers,* p. 135.

53. Ibid., p. 150.

3. The Original Following

1. However, some localized research can be—and has been—undertaken with data aggregated at a lower level.

2. A fourth study compares the working-class component of the Peronist vote in 1946 with that of 1973. See Darío Canton, Jorge Raúl Jorrat, and Eduardo Juárez, "Un intento de estimación de las celdas interiores de una tabla

de contingencia basado en el análisis de regresión," *Desarrollo Económico* 16 (1976), 395–417.

3. Peter Smith, "The Social Base of Peronism," *Hispanic American Historical Review* 52 (1972), 55–73.

4. Gino Germani, "El surgimiento del Peronismo: El rol de los obreros y de los migrantes internos," *Desarrollo Económico* 13 (1973), 435–488.

5. Peter Smith, "Las elecciones argentinas de 1946 y las inferencias ecológicas," *Desarrollo Económico* 14 (1974), 385–398.

6. E. Spencer Wellhofer, "The Mobilization of the Periphery: Perón's 1946 Triumph," *Comparative Political Studies* 7 (1974), 239–251. Works based on another empirical study which should be noted in passing: Lars Schoultz, "The Socioeconomic Determinants of Popular-Authoritarian Electoral Behavior: The Case of Peronism," *American Political Science Review* 71 (1977), 1423–1446, and *The Populist Challenge: Argentine Electoral Behavior in the Postwar Era* (Chapel Hill: University of North Carolina Press, 1983). Schoultz treats the 1946 Perón vote only peripherally, because his primary concern is with what might be called timeless Peronism—that is, the support Perón enjoyed constantly throughout the 1946–1973 period. Except for a few simple correlations for which 1946 data are used, there is little in these works which is germane to our investigation. (Indeed, the analytic strategy employed renders any investigation of change impossible.) Hence we will not speak to their strengths and weaknesses.

7. Smith, "The Social Base of Peronism," p. 67.

8. Germani, "El surgimiento del Peronismo," pp. 437–440, 443–444.

9. Wellhofer, "The Mobilization of the Periphery," pp. 248–249.

10. Smith, "The Social Base of Peronism," p. 70.

11. In his 1974 reply to Germani, Smith changed his indices of industrial and commercial blue-collar workers to the ratios of those workers to the adult male population, but the place of employment problem apparently remained unrecognized.

12. Darío Canton, *Materiales para el estudio de la sociología política en la Argentina* (Buenos Aires: Editorial del Instituto [Torcuato DiTella], 1968), pp. 152–153.

13. Richard J. Walter, *The Socialist Party of Argentina, 1890–1930* (Austin: University of Texas Press, 1977).

14. Germani, "El surgimiento del Peronismo," p. 437.

15. Gino Germani, "Mass Immigration and Modernization in Argentina," *Studies in Comparative International Development* 2 (1966), 173.

16. Germani, "El surgimiento del Peronismo," p. 452.

17. Smith, "Las elecciones argentinas," p. 389.

18. Smith, "The Social Base of Peronism," p. 73.

19. Germani, "El surgimiento del Peronismo," p. 445.

20. Wellhofer, "The Mobilization of the Periphery," p. 241.

21. See Mattei Dogan and Stein Rokkan, eds., *Quantitative Ecological Analysis in the Social Sciences* (Cambridge: MIT Press, 1969).

22. See Irwin Deutscher, ed., *What We Say/What We Do* (Glenview, Ill.: Scott Foresman, 1973).

23. Douglas Madsen and Peter G. Snow, "Perón and Peronism: The Routinization of Charisma," paper presented at the Eleventh World Congress of the International Political Science Association (1976).

24. Richard Nisbett and Lee Ross, *Human Inference: Strategies and Shortcomings of Social Judgment* (Englewood Cliffs, N.J.: Prentice-Hall, 1980).

25. Phillip E. Converse, "The Nature of Belief Systems in Mass Publics," in David Apter, ed., *Ideology and Discontent* (New York: Free Press, 1964), pp. 206–261, and Converse, "Attitudes and Non-Attitudes: Confirmation of a Dialogue," in Edward Tufte, ed., *The Quantitative Study of Politics* (New York: Addison-Wesley, 1971), pp. 168–189.

26. See W. S. Robinson, "Ecological Correlations and the Behavior of Individuals," *American Sociological Review* 15 (1950), 351–357; Leo A. Goodman, "Some Alternatives to Ecological Correlation," *American Journal of Sociology* 64 (1959), 610–625; W. Phillips Shively, " 'Ecological' Inference: The Use of Aggregate Data to Study Individuals," *American Political Science Review* 63 (1969), 1183–1196; Eric A. Hanushek, John E. Jackson, and John F. Kain, "Model Specification, Use of Aggregate Data, and the Ecological Correlation Fallacy," *Political Methodology* 1 (1974), 89–107; Christopher H. Achen, "Necessary and Sufficient Conditions for Unbiased Aggregation of Cross-Sectional Regressions," paper presented at the 1986 meeting of the American Political Science Association.

27. Donald E. Stokes, "Cross-Level Inference as a Game against Nature," in Joseph L. Bernd, ed., *Mathematical Applications in Political Science* (Charlottesville: University of Virginia Press, 1969), pp. 62–83.

28. Ibid., p. 62.

29. Hanushek, Jackson, and Kain, "Model Specification," and Christopher H. Achen, "Causal Specifications in Ecological Inference: The Search for Microfoundations," paper presented at the 1987 meeting of the Midwest Political Science Association.

30. See Eric M. Uslaner, "The Pitfalls of Per Capita," *American Journal of Political Science* 20 (1976), 125–133; Uslaner, "Straight Lines and Straight Thinking: Can All Those Econometricians Be Wrong?" *American Journal of Political Science* 21 (1977), 183–191; William G. Vanderbok, "On Improving the Analysis of Ratio Data," *Political Methodology* 4 (1977), 171–184; Adam Przeworski and Fernando Cortes, "Comparing Partial and Ratio Regression Models," *Political Methodology* 4 (1977), 63–75; and Karl Pearson, "On a Form of Spurious Correlation Which May Arise When Indices Are Used in

the Measurement of Organs," *Proceedings of the Royal Society of London* 60 (1897), 489–502.

31. Glen Firebaugh, "The Ratio Variables Hoax in Political Science," *American Journal of Political Science* 32 (1988), 523–535.

32. Ibid., p. 525.

33. William Lyons, "Per Capita Index Construction: A Defense," *American Journal of Political Science* 21 (1977), 177–182.

34. See Chapter 2.

35. Robert D. Crassweller, *Perón and the Enigmas of Argentina* (New York: W. W. Norton, 1987).

36. Joseph Page, *Perón: A Biography* (New York: Random House, 1983), p. 132.

37. We do not mean to claim that all attenders were passionate followers; surely some were present more out of curiosity than devotion.

38. Lars Schoultz, "A Diachronic Analysis of Peronist Electoral Behavior" (Ph.D. dissertation, University of North Carolina, 1973).

39. Angus Campbell, "Surge and Decline: A Study of Electoral Change," *Public Opinion Quarterly* 24 (1960), 40–62.

40. W. D. Burnham, *Critical Elections and the Mainsprings of American Politics* (New York: W. W. Norton, 1970).

41. Voting was not compulsory for those above the age of sixty-five or for persons who resided far from their polling place.

42. Galen Irwin, "Compulsory Voting Legislation: Impact on Voter Turnout in the Netherlands," *Comparative Political Studies* 7 (1974), 292–315.

43. The statistical analyses conducted here were done using the Minitab interactive software system. Minitab has plotting and regression-diagnostic capabilities which are especially useful in fitting statistical models to aggregate data.

44. As is often the case with ecological regression models, the error variance in the OLS version of this equation is not constant for all values of the independent variable. This condition violates an assumption of the statistical technique. See Michael Lewis-Beck, *Applied Regression: An Introduction* (Beverly Hills: Sage Publications, 1980), p. 28, and Eric A. Hanushek and John E. Jackson, *Statistical Methods for Social Scientists* (New York: Academic Press, 1977), pp. 150–153. Moreover, it invalidates the significance tests. Correction of this condition involves the use of weighted least squares (WLS) regression. The conventional practice in aggregate data analysis is to weight with some function of population size, the rationale being that smaller places are more idiosyncratic and therefore provide worse estimates of the underlying relationship, and that larger places are just the opposite. In order to determine the appropriate function we used a test suggested by Robert S. Pindycke and Daniel L. Rubinfeld, *Econometric Models and Economic Forecasts* (New York:

McGraw-Hill, 1981), p. 151. This test is satisfied when the absolute values of the residuals are not significantly related to the independent variable (here, population). We found that a weight factor equal to number of registrants, taken to the .7 power, satisfied this test in the analyses which follow. WLS regression does not calculate a coefficient of determination. We have estimated this coefficient by taking the square of the product moment correlation between actual and predicted dependent variables.

45. See Hanushek and Jackson, *Statistical Methods.*

46. Note that this model is multiplicative. Because the independent variables are logged, the true functional form is $P_L^* = 10^{B1} \times R_L^{B2} \times M_L^{B3} \times IO_L^{B4} \times 10^e$. In such a model the marginal effect of an independent variable depends not just on its value but also on the values of all other independent variables. For more information see Hanushek and Jackson, *Statistical Methods,* p. 98.

47. See Dogan and Rokkan, *Quantitative Ecological Analysis.*

48. Schoultz, "A Diachronic Analysis"; Schoultz, "The Socioeconomic Determinants"; and Schoultz, *The Populist Challenge.*

4. Dispersion of the Charismatic Response

1. Parts of this chapter are adapted from Douglas Madsen and Peter G. Snow, "Perón and Peronism: The Routinization of Charisma," paper presented at the Eleventh World Congress of the International Political Science Association, 1976; Madsen and Snow, "The Dispersion of Charisma," *Comparative Political Studies* 16 (1983), 337–362; and Madsen and Snow, "Recruitment Contrasts in a Divided Charismatic Movement," *American Political Science Review* 81 (1987), 233–238.

2. Persons living in the four southernmost provinces (Río Negro, Neuquén, Chubut, and Santa Cruz) were not sampled. At the time of the survey only about 3 percent of the nation's population lived in these provinces.

3. Jeane Kirkpatrick, *Leader and Vanguard in Mass Society: A Study of Peronist Argentina* (Cambridge: MIT Press, 1971), pp. 234–248.

4. In order to determine the point of affective neutrality in each of these measures, we examined the relationships between each measure and the neutral responses to the individual items which defined it. The neutral point for each dimension turned out to be very near the zero score, and thus in discussing these measures we equate positive scores with positive feelings and vice versa.

5. When Perón returned to Argentina in 1973 he demonstrated the persistence of his great appeal. One Argentine journalist, no friend of Perón, described the gathering of followers for the triumphal return as follows: "Four days before that date [of return] the area surrounding the stage [where Perón was to speak] was already besieged by men, women and children, old people, healthy and sick, able and disabled, blind and lame, who had come to listen

to the Lycurgus who had returned." Roberto Aizcorbe, *The Peronist Myth* (Hicksville, N.Y.: Exposition Press, 1975), p. 239. See also Joseph Page, *Perón: A Biography* (New York: Random House, 1983), pp. 462–466. The Argentine government estimated the size of the crowd at three million.

6. Where indices of any kind were created, the hypothesized relationships between items and the general domain they were thought to tap were tested both in the entire sample and in our Peronist subsets.

7. We constructed our index in such a manner to require not only that the respondent exhibit an agreement proclivity, but also that he or she do so when it involved contradicting the response to another related proposition. This could occur three times, and thus our score runs from zero to three. Note that a respondent could agree five times out of eight without any necessary contradiction; in such a case the acquiescence score would be zero.

8. Discriminant function coefficients (roughly analogous to Beta weights in regression analysis) are used for the former, and canonical correlations (comparable to multiple *R*s) for the latter. An alternative to discriminant analysis would have been to use probit analysis (but not OLS regression, since we have a dichotomous dependent variable). However, although the interpretation of individual variable weights would have been essentially the same, we chose discriminant analysis because it permits easy examination of asymmetry in the explanation of group identification. On discriminant analysis, see William W. Cooley and Paul R. Lohnes, *Multivariate Data Analysis* (New York: Wiley, 1971). On probit and discriminant analysis, see John Aldrich and Charles F. Cnudde, "Probing the Bounds of Conventional Wisdom: A Comparison of Regression, Probit, and Discriminant Analysis," *American Journal of Political Science* 19 (1975), 571–608.

9. The coding procedures utilized by the original investigator do not allow us to determine which union a respondent belonged to. We also are unable to determine whether it was a Peronist-controlled union.

10. Carlos F. Díaz Alejandro, *Essays on the Economic History of the Argentine Republic* (New Haven: Yale University Press, 1970), pp. 365, 459, 460, 527.

11. The group means presented in Table 4.2, as well as those in the following tables, are based on standardized variables. In each case the mean for the entire sample is zero. The means for our subgroups, then, represent units of deviation from the grand means. It thus is possible to compare each subgroup with the other and with the sample as a whole; moreover, this technique permits comparison of both continuous and categoric variables on the same basis.

12. In examining the means for each of the components of our summary class measure, it is interesting to note that while the Organization group is about 20 points below the national average in interviewer-appraised class and in other *objective* class terms, it is much lower in *subjective* class terms. In the latter instance it is much closer to the Personalists. This suggests that a residue

of working-class feeling has persisted even though lower middle-class circumstances have been attained.

13. Charles Cell, "Charismatic Heads of State: The Social Context," *Behavioral Science Research* 9 (1974), 274.

14. Although it is true that 50 percent of either group membership might be classified by chance, the reader is cautioned against simply subtracting 50 percent from the total correctly classified in order to determine the percentage correctly classified by means other than chance. When there are only two classification categories the percentage correctly classified by chance is the same as the percentage incorrectly classified, and thus in the case where 76 percent of the Personalists were correctly classified, 24 percent were a result of random successes and the remaining 52 percent were correctly classified on the basis of the socioeconomic variables employed. The general formula for determining the percentage correctly classified as a result of nonrandom factors (that is, the variables employed) is: $CC_{nr} = CC_t - (IC/n - 1C)$, where CC_{nr} is the percentage of correct classifications that are nonrandom; CC_t is the total percentage of correct classifications; IC is the percentage of incorrect classifications; and $n - 1C$ is the number of classification categories minus one. In cases such as ours, where the dependent variable is dichotomous, a simple way to determine the percentage of correct classifications which are *not* a result of chance is to subtract 100 from double the percentage of correct classifications. In the above case $(76 \times 2) - 100 = 52$.

15. Paul Allen Beck, "A Socialization Theory of Partisan Realignment," in Richard Niemi and Herbert Weisberg, eds., *Controversies in American Voting Behavior* (San Francisco: W. H. Freeman), pp. 396–411; Sidney Verba, Norman Nie, and Jae-on Kim, *Participation and Political Equality: A Seven-Nation Comparison* (London: Cambridge University Press, 1978).

16. Hadley Cantril, *Patterns of Human Concerns* (New Brunswick, N.J.: Rutgers University Press, 1965).

17. See Daniel James, "The Peronist Left, 1955–1975," *Journal of Latin American Studies* 8 (1976), 273–296, and James, *Resistance and Integration: Peronism and the Argentine Working Class* (New York: Cambridge University Press, 1988).

18. This condition is given theoretical discussion and clear illustration in Roger Brown, *Social Psychology: The Second Edition* (New York: Free Press, 1965), pp. 549–609.

19. Díaz Alejandro, *Essays,* p. 538.

20. See Guido DiTella, *Argentina under Perón* (New York: St. Martin's Press, 1983), chap. 2; Richard Gillespie, *Soldiers of Perón: Argentina's Montoneros* (Oxford: Oxford University Press, 1982); Roberto Güimaraes, "Understanding Support for Terrorism through Survey Data," in Frederick C. Turner and José Enrique Miguens, eds., *Juan Perón and the Reshaping of Argentina*

(Pittsburgh: Pittsburgh University Press, 1982), pp. 189–222; Page, *Perón*, chap. 47; and Wayne Smith, "The Return of Peronism," in Turner and Miguens, *Juan Perón*, pp. 97–146.

21. It was not until the very late 1960s that Perón began to give some moral support to left radicals within his movement.

22. Unlike their older counterparts, the Personalist and Organizational youth are farther apart in terms of their attitudes than in terms of socioeconomic location. A discriminant function analysis of socio-economic location variables produces a canonical correlation of .43 and correctly classifies 71 percent of the youth; the nine attitudinal measures produce a canonical correlation of .59 and correctly classify 80 percent.

23. James March, "Some Recent Substantive and Methodological Developments in the Theory of Organizational Decision-Making," in Austin Ranney, ed., *Essays in the Behavioral Study of Politics* (Urbana: University of Illinois Press, 1962), p. 194.

5. The Residue of Charisma

1. Darío Canton, *El pueblo legislador: Las elecciones de 1983* (Buenos Aires: Centro Editor de América Latina, 1986). On the sample, see pp. 238–240.

2. In the 1983 presidential election in the Federal Capital the Peronist candidate received 29.6 percent of the male vote and 25.6 percent of the female vote. For the election results by ward see María Teresa Farrés, Jorge A. Jaroslavsky, and Emilio Fermín Mignone, *Elecciones y participación* (Buenos Aires: COPEDE, 1984), pp. 41–95. It should be remembered that in Argentina men and women vote in separate places, and official figures are kept by sex.

3. Canton, *El pueblo legislador*, p. 160.

4. Ibid., p. 165.

5. Some of these people probably cast "antimilitary" votes both in 1973 and in 1983. In the former year the best way to repudiate the outgoing military regime was to vote Peronist. In his memoir General Alejandro Lanusse says that many people voted against him rather than for Cámpora. See Alejandro Lanusse, *Mi testimonio* (Buenos Aires: Lesserre Editores, 1977), p. 272. A decade later it was the Radicals, and especially Alfonsín, who wore the antimilitary mantle; late in the campaign there were even rumors of an agreement by the Peronists not to try military personnel for alleged abuses committed during the "dirty war." (In 1989, shortly after Peronism returned to power, President Carlos Saúl Menem issued a general amnesty for those military men convicted of human rights abuses between 1976 and 1983.)

6. For details on the selection of these precincts see Peter G. Snow, *Political Forces in Argentina* (New York: Praeger Special Editions, 1979), pp. 34–40.

7. Although all Peronist leaders had to pay lip service to the notion that

Justicialismo was the formal ideology of Peronism, it clearly was no ideology at all.

8. In his last public speech Perón said, "My only heir is the people." See Daniel Poneman, *Argentina: Democracy on Trial* (New York: Paragon House, 1987), p. 77.

9. This observation is based on conversations by one of the authors with an unsystematic sample of Argentines during the week immediately preceding the 1983 elections.

10. Carlos Grasso, comments on Luis González Esteves and Ignacio Llorente, "Elecciones y preferencias políticas en la Capital Federal y Gran Buenos Aires: El 30 de octubre de 1983," in *La Argentina electoral* (Buenos Aires: Editorial Sudamericana, 1985), p. 79.

11. Esteves and Llorente, "Elecciones," p. 55.

12. Ibid., p. 59.

13. Ibid., p. 65.

14. Gary Wynia, *Argentina: Illusions and Reality* (New York: Holmes and Meier, 1986), p. 182.

15. Cámara de Diputados, *diario de sesiones,* February 10–11, 1984 cited by Liliana de Riz, "Alfonsín's Argentina: Renewal of Parties and Congress" (mimeo, July 1988), p. 9. Similar sentiment was expressed after the election of Menem, when the leader of the Metalworkers Union said that the unions had turned the movement over to politicians who proved to be incapable of dealing with national problems. He went on to say, "What have they [Peronist politicians] done with Perón's movement? They have carried it to chaos. Thus we [the unions], the backbone of Peronism, must contribute to the re-creation of the Justicialist Movement." See *El informador público* (Buenos Aires), March 16, 1990, p. 8.

16. Menem won 88.7 percent of the vote in San Juan, 98.5 percent in Catamarca, and 98.6 percent in his own province of La Rioja.

17. Salaries lost almost half their purchasing power during the Radical administration, and in the three months preceding the election the national monetary unit, the austral, had gone from 17 to the dollar to 180.

18. Due to overrepresentation of the smaller, poorer provinces in the electoral college, Menem received 310 of the 600 electoral votes.

19. Quoted in "Carlos Menem defiende el indulto," *Proceso* (Buenos Aires), October 30, 1989, p. 42.

20. This may be a bit overstated for today's world. In advanced industrial societies the communications networks which penetrate societies have the capacity to aggregate troubled individuals, previously too scattered across the landscape to be thought of as a collective body, into a mass which is both ripe for charismatic bonding and large enough to have political significance. Still, the absence of shoulder-to-shoulder interaction would seem likely to mute collective consciousness and consequently the behavior of such an audience.

21. Pertinent evidence can be found in Patricia Gurin and Orville G. Brim, Jr., "Change in Self in Adulthood: The Example of Sense of Control," *Life-Span Development and Behavior* 6 (1984), 282–334, and Douglas Madsen, "Political Self-Efficacy Tested," *American Political Science Review* 81 (1987), 571–581.

22. Of course, even in moderate change there may be pockets of crisis; some organizations may die when an economy has only caught cold. Although there is a collectivity involved here and, in fact, a localized charismatic bond may develop under the right conditions, these events are of insufficient scope to translate into the what we are calling political charisma—that which shakes entire societies.

23. Gabriel Almond and Sidney Verba, *The Civic Culture: Political Attitudes and Democracy in Five Nations* (Boston: Little, Brown, 1965).

24. Carlos Díaz Alejandro, *Essays on the Economic History of the Argentine Republic* (New Haven: Yale University Press, 1970).

25. Muzafer Sherif, "Experiments in Group Conflict," in Stanley Coopersmith, ed., *Frontiers of Psychological Research* (San Francisco: W. H. Freeman, 1966), pp. 112–116.

26. See Michael S. Lewis-Beck and Peveril Squire, "The Transformation of the American State: The New Era–New Deal Test" (manuscript, 1988).

27. Martin McCauley and Stephen Carter, "Introduction," in McCauley and Carter, eds., *Leadership and Succession in the Soviet Union, Eastern Europe, and China* (Armonk, N.Y.: M. E. Sharpe, 1986), p. 1.

Bibliography

Abel, Theodore. *The Nazi Movement*. New York: Atherton, 1965.

Achen, Christopher H. "Causal Specifications in Ecological Inference: The Search for Microfoundations." Paper presented at the 1987 meeting of the Midwest Political Science Association.

———. "Necessary and Sufficient Conditions for Unbiased Aggregation of Cross-Sectional Regressions." Paper presented at the 1986 meeting of the American Political Science Association.

Aizcorbe, Roberto. *The Peronist Myth*. Hicksville, N.Y.: Exposition Press, 1975.

Aldrich, John, and Charles F. Cnudde. "Probing the Bounds of Conventional Wisdom: A Comparison of Regression, Probit, and Discriminant Analysis." *American Journal of Political Science* 19 (1975): 571–608.

Almond, Gabriel A., and Sidney Verba. *Civic Culture: Political Attitudes and Democracy in Five Nations*. Boston: Little, Brown, 1965.

Andino, Ramón, and Eduardo J. Paredes. *Breve historia de los partidos políticos argentinos*. Buenos Aires: Alzamor Editores, 1974.

Apter, David, ed. *Ideology and Discontent*. New York: Free Press, 1964.

Archer, John. *Animals under Stress*. Baltimore: University Park Press, 1979.

Bandura, Albert. "Self-Efficacy: Toward a Unifying Theory of Behavioral Change." *Psychological Review* 84 (1977): 191–215.

———. "Self-Efficacy Mechanism in Human Agency." *American Psychologist* 37 (1982): 122–147.

———. *Social Foundations of Thought and Action*. Englewood Cliffs, N.J.: Prentice-Hall, 1986.

Beck, Paul Allen. "A Socialization Theory of Partisan Realignment." In Richard Niemi and Herbert Weisberg, eds., *Controversies in American Voting Behavior*, pp. 396–411. San Francisco: W. H. Freeman, 1976.

Berkowitz, Leonard, ed. *Advances in Experimental Social Psychology*. Vol. 14. New York: Academic Press, 1981.

Bernd, Joseph L. *Mathematical Applications in Political Science.* Charlottesville: University of Virginia Press, 1969.

Bion, W. R. *Attention and Interpretation.* London: Tavistock, 1970.

Blake, Robert, and Jane Mouton. "Reactions to Intergroup Competition under Win-Lose Conditions." *Management Science* 7 (1961): 420–435.

Brown, Roger. *Social Psychology: The Second Edition.* New York: Free Press, 1985.

Burnham, W. D. *Critical Elections and the Mainsprings of American Politics.* New York: W. W. Norton, 1970.

Calvert, Susan, and Peter Calvert. *Argentina: Political Culture and Instability.* Pittsburgh: University of Pittsburgh Press, 1989.

Campbell, Angus. "Surge and Decline: A Study of Electoral Change." *Public Opinion Quarterly* 24 (1960): 40–62.

Canton, Darío. *Elecciones y partidos políticos en la Argentina.* Buenos Aires: Siglo Veintiuno Argentina Editores, 1973.

———. *Materiales para el estudio de la sociología política en la Argentina.* Buenos Aires: Editorial del Instituto [Torcuato DiTella], 1968.

———. *El pueblo legislador: Las elecciones de 1983.* Buenos Aires: Centro Editor de América Latina, 1986.

Canton, Darío, Jorge Raúl Jorrat, and Eduardo Juárez. "Un intento de estimación de las celdas interiores de una tabla de contingencia basado en el análisis de regresión: El caso de las elecciones presidenciales de 1946 y marzo de 1973." *Desarrollo Económico* 16 (1976): 395–417.

Cantril, Hadley. *Patterns of Human Concerns.* New Brunswick, N.J.: Rutgers University Press, 1965.

———. *The Politics of Despair.* New York: Collier, 1958.

Carri, Roberto. *Sindicatos y poder en la Argentina.* Buenos Aires: Editorial Sudestada, 1967.

Catterberg, Edgardo Raúl. "Las elecciones del 30 de octubre de 1983: El surgimiento de una nueva convergencia electoral." *Desarrollo Económico* 25 (July-September 1985): 259–267.

Cavarozzi, Marcelo. "Peronism and Radicalism: Argentina's Transitions in Perspective." In Paul W. Drake and Eduardo Silva, eds., *Elections and Democratization in Latin America, 1980–85,* pp. 143–174. San Diego: Center for Iberian and Latin American Studies, 1986.

———. "Political Cycles in Argentina since 1955." In Guillermo O'Donnell, Philippe C. Schmitter, and Laurence Whitehead, eds., *Transitions from Authoritarian Rule: Latin America,* pp. 19–48. Baltimore: Johns Hopkins University Press, 1986.

Cavarozzi, Marcelo, and María Grossi. "From Democratic Reinvention to Political Decline and Hyperinflation The Argentina of Alfonsín." Paper presented at the Fifteenth Congress of the Latin American Studies Association, Miami, December 1989.

Cell, Charles. "Charismatic Heads of State: The Social Context." *Behavioral Science Research* 9 (1974): 255–306.

Converse, Phillip E. "Attitudes and Non-Attitudes: Confirmation of a Dialogue." In Edward Tufte, ed., *The Quantitative Study of Politics*, pp. 168–189. Reading, Mass.: Addison-Wesley, 1971.

————. "The Nature of Belief Systems in Mass Publics." In David Apter, ed., *Ideology and Discontent*, pp. 206–261. New York: Free Press, 1964.

————. "Of Time and Partisan Stability." *Comparative Political Studies* 2 (1969): 139–171.

Cooley, William W., and Paul R. Lohnes. *Multivariate Data Analysis*. New York: Wiley, 1971.

Coopersmith, Stanley, ed. *Frontiers of Psychological Research*. San Francisco: W. H. Freeman, 1966.

Cornblit, Oscar. "Inmigrantes y empresarios en la política argentina." In Torcuato DiTella and Tulio Halperín Donghi, eds., *Los fragmentos del poder*, pp. 389–438. Buenos Aires: Editorial Jorge Alvarez, 1969.

Corradi, Juan E. *The Fitful Republic: Economy, Society, and Politics in Argentina*. Boulder: Westview Press, 1985.

Crassweller, Robert D. *Perón and the Enigmas of Argentina*. New York: W. W. Norton, 1987.

Crossman, Richard. *The God That Failed*. New York: Harper, 1949.

Cyert, Richard M., and Kenneth R. MacCrimmon. "Organizations." In Gardner Lindzay and Elliot Aronson, eds., *Handbook of Social Psychology*, vol. 1, pp. 568–614. Reading, Mass.: Addison-Wesley, 1969.

d'Abate, Juan Carlos. "Trade Unions and Peronism." In Frederick C. Turner and José Enrique Miguens, eds., *Juan Perón and the Reshaping of Argentina*, pp. 55–78. Pittsburgh: Pittsburgh University Press, 1983.

Dahl, Robert A. *Modern Political Analysis*. 4th ed. Englewood Cliffs, N.J.: Prentice-Hall, 1984.

————. *Polyarchy: Participation and Opposition*. New Haven: Yale University Press, 1971.

————. "Power." In David L. Sills, ed., *International Encyclopedia of the Social Sciences*, vol. 12, pp. 405–415. New York: Free Press, 1968.

Davies, James C. "Charisma in the 1952 Campaign." *American Political Science Review* 48 (1954): 1083–1102.

Deutscher, Irwin, ed. *What We Say/What We Do*. Glenview, Ill.: Scott Foresman, 1973.

Díaz Alejandro, Carlos. *Essays on the Economic History of the Argentine Republic*. New Haven: Yale University Press, 1970.

Dirección Nacional de Estadística y Censos. *Segundo censo de la República Argentina*. Buenos Aires: n.p., 1898.

DiTella, Guido. *Argentina under Perón*. New York: St. Martin's Press, 1983.

Dogan, Mattei, and Stein Rokkan, eds. *Quantitative Ecological Analysis in the Social Sciences.* Cambridge: MIT Press, 1969.

Drake, Paul W., and Eduardo Silva, eds. *Elections and Democratization in Latin America, 1980–85.* San Diego: Center for Iberian and Latin American Studies, 1986.

Edwards, Christopher. *Crazy for God.* Englewood Cliffs, N.J.: Prentice-Hall, 1979.

Errandonea h., Alfredo. "Algunas hipótesis sobre el cambio sociopolítico en la Argentina actual." In Daniel García Deleado, ed., *Los cambios en la sociedad política,* pp. 11–29. Buenos Aires: Centro Editor de América Latina, 1987.

Esteves, Luis González, and Ignacio Llorente. "Elecciones y preferencias políticas en Capital Federal y Gran Buenos Aires: El 30 de octubre de 1983." *La Argentina electoral,* pp. 39–73. Buenos Aires: Editorial Sudamericana, 1985.

Farrés, María Teresa, Jorge A. Jaroslavsky, and Emilio Mignone. *Elecciones y participación.* Buenos Aires: COPEDE, 1984.

Firebaugh, Glen, "The Ratio Variables Hoax in Political Science." *American Journal of Political Science* 32 (1988), 523–535.

Ford, A. G. "British Investment and Argentine Economic Development, 1880–1914." In David Rock, ed., *Argentina in the Twentieth Century,* pp. 12–40. Pittsburgh: University of Pittsburgh Press, 1975.

Fraser, Nicolas and Marysa Navarro. *Eva Perón.* New York: W. W. Norton, 1980.

Germani, Gino. *La estructura social de la Argentina.* Buenos Aires: Editorial Raigal, 1955.

———. "Mass Immigration and Modernization in Argentina." *Studies in Comparative International Development.* 2 (1966): 163–182.

———. "El surgimiento del Peronismo: el rol de los obreros y de los migrantes internos." *Desarrollo Económico* 13 (1973): 435–488.

Gibb, Cecil A. "Leadership." In Gardner Lindzay and Elliot Aronson, eds., *Handbook of Social Psychology,* vol. 1, 568–614. Reading, Mass.: Addison-Wesley, 1969.

Gillespie, Richard. *Soldiers of Perón: Argentina's Montoneros.* London: Oxford University Press, 1982.

Goldwert, Marvin. "Dichotomies of Militarism in Argentina." *Orbis* 10 (1966): 930–939.

Goodman, Leo A. "Some Alternatives to Ecological Correlations." *American Journal of Sociology* 64 (1959): 610–625.

Gouldner, Alvin W. "Introduction," in Gouldner, ed., *Studies in Leadership,* pp. 21–31. New York: Harper and Brothers, 1950.

Greenup, Ruth, and Leonard Greenup. *Revolution before Breakfast.* Chapel Hill: University of North Carolina Press, 1945.

Gregor, James A. "Fascism: The Contemporary Interpretations." University Programs Modular Studies. Morristown, N.J.: General Learning Press, 1973.

Guardo, Ricardo C. *Horas difíciles*. Buenos Aires: Ediciones Ricardo C. Guardo, 1963.

Güimaraes, Roberto. "Understanding Support for Terrorism through Survey Data." In Frederick C. Turner and José Enrique Miguens, eds., *Juan Perón and the Reshaping of Argentina*, pp. 189–222. Pittsburgh: Pittsburgh University Press, 1983.

Gurin, Patricia, and Orville G. Brim, Jr. "Change in Self in Adulthood: The Example of Sense of Control." *Life-Span Development and Behavior* 6 (1984): 282–334.

Hamblin, Robert. "Group Integration during a Crisis." *Human Relations* 11 (1958): 67–76.

———. "Leadership and Crises." *Sociometry* 21 (1958): 322–335.

Hamilton, Victoria. "Some Problems in the Clinical Application of Attachment Theory." *Psychoanalytic Psychotherapy* 3 (1987): 67–83.

Hanushek, Eric A., and John E. Jackson. *Statistical Methods for Social Scientists*. New York: Academic Press, 1977.

Hanushek, Eric A., John E. Jackson, and John F. Kain. "Model Specification, Use of Aggregate Data, and the Ecological Correlation Fallacy." *Political Methodology* 1 (1974): 89–107.

Heclo, Hugh. "Introduction: The Presidential Illusion." In Hugh Heclo and Lester Salaman, eds., *The Illusion of Presidential Government*, pp. 1–17. Boulder: Westview Press, 1981.

Helmreich, R. L., and B. E. Collins. "Situational Determinants of Affiliative Preferences under Stress." *Journal of Personality and Social Psychology* 6 (1957): 79–85.

Henderson, A. M., and Talcott Parsons, eds. *The Theory of Social and Economic Organization*. New York: Oxford University Press, 1974.

Hodges, Donald C. *Argentina, 1943–1976: The National Revolution and Resistance*. Albuquerque: University of New Mexico Press, 1976.

Hogg, Michael A., and Dominic Abrams. *Social Identifications*. New York: Routledge, 1988.

Irwin, Galen. "Compulsory Voting Legislation: Impact on Voter Turnout in the Netherlands." *Comparative Political Studies* 7 (1974): 292–315.

James, Daniel. "17 y 18 de octubre de 1945: El Peronismo, la protesta de masas y la clase obrera argentina." *Desarrollo Económico* 27 (1987): 445–461.

———. "The Peronist Left, 1955–1975." *Journal of Latin American Studies* 8 (1976): 273–296.

———. *Resistance and Integration: Peronism and the Argentine Working Class, 1946–1976*. New York: Cambridge University Press, 1988.

Janis, Irving L. *Victims of Groupthink*. Boston: Houghton Mifflin, 1972.

Janowitz, Morris, and Dwaine Marvick. "Authoritarianism and Political Behavior." *Public Opinion Quarterly* 17 (1953): 185–201.

Jennings, M. Kent. "Residues of a Movement: The Aging of the American Protest Generation." *American Political Science Review* 81 (1987): 367–382.

Kelley, H. H., et al. "Collective Behavior in a Simulated Panic Situation." *Journal of Experimental Social Psychology* 1 (1965): 20–54.

Kinder, Donald R. "Presidential Prototypes." *Political Behavior* 2 (1982): 315–337.

Kirkpatrick, Jeane. *Leader and Vanguard in Mass Society: A Study of Peronist Argentina*. Cambridge: MIT Press, 1971.

Koestler, Arthur. "The Initiates." In Richard Crossman, ed., *The God That Failed*, pp. 15–75. New York: Harper, 1949.

Kornhauser, William. *The Politics of Mass Society*. New York: Free Press, 1959.

Lane, Robert E. *Political Ideology*. New York: Free Press, 1962.

Lanusse, Alejandro. *Mi testimonio*. Buenos Aires: Lasserre Editores, 1977.

Lanzetta, J. T. "Group Behavior under Stress." *Human Relations* 8 (1955): 29–52.

Lasswell, Harold. *Power and Personality*. New York: Viking Press, 1948.

Lewis, Paul H. *The Crisis of Argentine Capitalism*. Chapel Hill: University of North Carolina Press, 1990.

Lewis-Beck, Michael S. *Applied Regression: An Introduction*. Beverly Hills: Sage Publications, 1980.

Lewis-Beck, Michael S., and Peverill Squire. "The Transformation of the American State: New Era–New Deal Test." Manuscript, 1988.

Liff, Zanvel A. *The Leader in the Group*. New York: Jason Aronson, 1975.

Lindzay, Gardner, and Elliot Aronson, eds. *Handbook of Social Psychology*. Vol. 1. Reading, Mass.: Addison-Wesley, 1969.

Lipset, S. M., and Stein Rokkan, eds. *Party Systems and Voter Alignments*. New York: Free Press, 1967.

Luna, Félix. *Argentina de Perón a Lanusse, 1943–73*. Barcelona: Editorial Planeta, 1972.

———. *Diálogos con Frondizi*. Buenos Aires: Editorial Desarrollo, 1963.

———. *El 45*. Buenos Aires: Editorial Jorge Alvarez, 1969.

Lyons, William. "Per Capita Index Construction: A Defense." *American Journal of Political Science* 21 (1977): 177–182.

MacDonald, Austin F. *Latin American Politics and Government*. New York: Thomas Y. Crowell, 1954.

McCauley, Martin, and Stephen Carter, eds. *Leadership and Succession in the Soviet Union, Eastern Europe, and China*. Armonk, N.Y.: M. E. Sharpe, 1986.

Madsen, Douglas. "Political Information Processing in an Electoral Context." *International Political Science Review* 2 (1981): 423–443.

———. "Political Self-Efficacy Tested." *American Political Science Review* 81 (1987): 571–581.

Madsen, Douglas, and Peter G. Snow. "The Dispersion of Charisma." *Comparative Political Studies* 16 (1983): 337–362.

———. "Perón and Peronism: The Routinization of Charisma." Paper presented at the Eleventh World Congress of the International Political Science Association, 1976.

———. "Recruitment Contrasts in a Divided Charismatic Movement." *American Political Science Review* 81 (1987): 233–238.

March, James. "Some Recent Substantive and Methodological Developments in the Theory of Organizational Decision-Making." In Austin Ranney, ed., *Essays in the Behavioral Study of Politics,* pp. 191–208. Urbana: University of Illinois Press, 1962.

Marvick, Dwaine. "Party Cadres and Receptive Party Voters in the 1967 Indian National Election." *Asian Survey* 10 (1970): 949–966.

Merkl, Peter. *The Making of a Storm Trooper.* Princeton, N.J.: Princeton University Press, 1980.

———. *Political Violence under the Swastika: 581 Early Nazis.* Princeton, N.J.: Princeton University Press, 1975.

Miguens, José Enrique. "The Presidential Elections of 1973 and the End of Ideology." In Frederick C. Turner and José Enrique Miguens, eds., *Juan Perón and the Reshaping of Argentina,* pp. 147–170. Pittsburgh: University of Pittsburgh Press, 1983.

Miller, Arthur A., et al. "Schematic Assessments of Presidential Candidates." *American Political Science Review* 80 (1986): 521–540.

Miller, Suzanne M. "Predictability and Human Stress: Towards a Clarification of Evidence and Theory." In Leonard Berkowitz, ed., *Advances in Experimental Social Psychology,* vol.14, pp. 203–256.New York: Academic Press, 1981.

Ministerio del Interior, Departamento Electoral. "Elección de Diputados Nacionales, 14-III-1965: Resultados por distrito." Mimeo.

Most, Benjamin A. "Authoritarianism and the Growth of the State: An Assessment of Their Impact on Argentine Public Policy, 1930–1970." *Comparative Political Studies* 13 (1980): 173–203.

Neumann, Franz. *The Democratic and Authoritarian State.* New York: Free Press, 1957.

Niemi, Richard, and Herbert Weisberg, eds. *Controversies in American Voting Behavior.* San Francisco: W. H. Freeman, 1976.

Nisbett, Richard, and Lee Ross. *Human Inference: Strategies and Shortcomings of Social Judgment.* Englewood Cliffs, N.J.: Prentice-Hall, 1980.

O'Donnell, Guillermo. *Bureaucratic Authoritarianism: Argentina, 1966–1973, in Comparative Perspective*. Berkeley: University of California Press, 1988.

O'Donnell, Guillermo, Philippe C. Schmitter, and Laurence Whitehead, eds. *Transitions from Authoritarian Rule: Latin America*. Baltimore: Johns Hopkins University Press, 1986.

Oyhanarte, Julio. "Historia del poder judicial." *Todo es Historia* 6 (1972): 86–121.

Page, Joseph. *Perón: A Biography*. New York: Random House, 1983.

Pearson, Karl. "On a Form of Spurious Correlation Which May Arise When Indices Are Used in the Measurement of Organs." *Proceedings of the Royal Society of London* 60 (1897): 489–502.

Peralta Ramos, Mónica, and Carlos H. Waisman, eds. *From Military Rule to Liberal Democracy in Argentina*. Boulder: Westview Press, 1987.

Perón, Eva. *My Mission in Life*. New York: Vantage Press, 1953.

Pindyke, Robert S., and Daniel L. Rubinfeld. *Econometric Models and Economic Forecasts*. New York: McGraw-Hill, 1981.

Poneman, Daniel. *Argentina: Democracy on Trial*. New York: Paragon House, 1987.

Przeworski, Adam, and Fernando Cortes. "Comparing Partial and Ratio Regression Models." *Political Methodology* 4 (1977): 63–75.

Puiggrós, Rodolfo. *La democracia fraudulenta*. Buenos Aires: Editorial Jorge Alvarez, 1968.

Randall, Laura. *An Economic History of Argentina in the Twentieth Century*. New York: Columbia University Press, 1978.

Ranney, Austin, ed. *Essays in the Behavioral Study of Politics*. Urbana: University of Illinois Press, 1962.

Ratier, Hugo E. *Villeros y villas miserias*. Buenos Aires: Centro Editor de América Latina, 1971.

Renner, John, and Vivian Renner. "Effects of Stress on Group versus Individual Problem Solving." *Psychological Reports* 30 (1972): 487–491.

Rennie, Ysabel. *The Argentine Republic*. New York: Macmillan, 1945.

Riz, Liliana de. "Alfonsín's Argentina: The Renewal of Parties and Congress." Mimeo, July 1988.

Robinson, W. S. "Ecological Correlations and the Behavior of Individuals." *American Sociological Review* 15 (1950): 351–357.

Rock, David. *Politics in Argentina, 1890–1930: The Rise and Fall of Radicalism*. London: Cambridge University Press, 1975.

————, ed. *Argentina in the Twentieth Century*. Pittsburgh: Pittsburgh University Press, 1975.

Romero, José Luis. *A History of Argentine Political Thought*. Stanford: Stanford University Press, 1963.

Rosenbaum, Leonard L., and William B. Rosenbaum. "Moral and Productivity

Consequences of Group Leadership Style, Stress, and Type of Task." *Journal of Applied Psychology* 55 (1971): 343–348.

Schachter, Stanley. *The Psychology of Affiliation*. Stanford: Stanford University Press, 1959.

Schiffer, Irvine. *Charisma: A Psychoanalytic Look at Mass Society*. Toronto: University of Toronto Press, 1973.

Schoultz, Lars. "A Diachronic Analysis of Peronist Electoral Behavior." Ph.D. dissertation, University of North Carolina, 1973.

———. *The Populist Challenge: Argentine Electoral Behavior in the Postwar Era*. Chapel Hill: University of North Carolina Press, 1983.

———. "The Socioeconomic Determinants of Popular-Authoritarian Electoral Behavior: The Case of Peronism." *American Political Science Review* 71 (1977): 1423–1446.

Sherif, Muzafer, et al. *Intergroup Conflict and Cooperation: The Robber's Cave Experiment*. Norman, Okla.: University Book Exchange, 1960.

———. "Experiments in Group Conflict." In Stanley Coopersmith, ed., *Frontiers of Psychological Research*, pp. 112–116. San Francisco: W. H. Freeman, 1966.

Shils, Edward. "Charisma, Order, and Status." *American Sociological Review* 30 (1965): 199–213.

———. "The Concentration and Dispersion of Charisma: Their Bearing on Economic Policy in Underdeveloped Countries." *World Politics* 11 (1958): 1–19.

———. "The Theory of Mass Society." *Diogenes* 39 (1962): 45–66.

Shils, Edward, and Morris Janowitz. "Cohesion and Disintegration in the *Wehrmacht* in World War II." *Public Opinion Quarterly* 12 (1948): 280–315.

Shively, W. Phillips. " 'Ecological' Inference: The Use of Aggregate Data to Study Individuals." *American Political Science Review* 63 (1969): 1183–1196.

Sills, David L., ed. *International Encyclopedia of the Social Sciences*. Vol. 12. New York: Free Press, 1968.

Simon, Herbert A. *Administrative Behavior*. New York: Free Press, 1976.

Simonton, Dean Keith. *Genius, Creativity, and Leadership: Historiometric Inquiries*. Cambridge: Harvard University Press, 1984.

Smith, Peter. "Las elecciones argentinas de 1946 y las inferencias ecológicas." *Desarrollo Económico* 14 (1974): 385–398.

———. "The Social Base of Peronism." *Hispanic American Historical Review* 52 (1972): 55–73.

Smith, Wayne. "The Return of Peronism." In Frederick C. Turner and José Enrique Miguens, eds., *Juan Perón and the Reshaping of Argentina*, pp. 97–146. Pittsburgh: Pittsburgh University Press, 1983.

Snow, Peter G. *Argentine Radicalism: The History and Doctrine of the Radical Civic Union*. Iowa City: University of Iowa Press, 1965.

———. "The Class Basis of Argentine Political Parties." *American Political Science Review* 63 (1969): 163–167.

———. *Political Forces in Argentina*. New York: Praeger Special Editions, 1979.

Stokes, Donald E. "Cross-Level Inference as a Game against Nature." In Joseph L. Bernd, ed., *Mathematical Applications in Political Science*, pp. 62–83. Charlottesville: University of Virginia Press, 1969.

Stouffer, Samuel, et al. *The American Soldier*. Princeton, N.J.: Princeton University Press, 1949.

Strümpfer, D. J. W. "Fear and Anxiety during a Disaster." *Journal of Social Psychology* 82 (1970): 263–268.

Szulc, Tad. *Twilight of the Tyrants*. New York: Henry Holt, 1959.

Tajfel, Henri. *Human Groups and Social Categories*. Cambridge: Cambridge University Press, 1981.

Tajfel, Henri, and J. C. Turner. "An Integrative Theory of Social Conflict." In W. Austin and S. Worchel, eds., *The Social Psychology of Intergroup Relations*, pp. 33–47. Monterey, Calif.: Brooks/Cole, 1979.

Tamarin, David. *The Argentine Labor Movement, 1930–1945: A Study in the Origins of Peronism*. Albuquerque: University of New Mexico Press, 1985.

Taylor, J. M. *Eva Perón: The Myths of a Woman*. Chicago: University of Chicago Press, 1979.

Tufte, Edward, ed. *The Quantitative Study of Politics*. Reading, Mass.: Addison-Wesley, 1971.

Turner, Frederick C., and José Enrique Miguens, eds. *Juan Perón and the Reshaping of Argentina*. Pittsburgh: Pittsburgh University Press, 1983.

Uslaner, Eric M. "The Pitfalls of Per Capita." *American Journal of Political Science* 20 (1976): 125–133.

———. "Straight Lines and Straight Thinking: Can All Those Econometricians Be Wrong?" *American Journal of Political Science* 21 (1977): 183–191.

Vanderbok, William G. "On Improving the Analysis of Ratio Data." *Political Methodology* 4 (1977): 171–184.

Verba, Sidney, Norman Nie, and Jae-on Kim. *Participation and Political Equality: A Seven-Nation Comparison*. London: Cambridge University Press, 1978.

Waisman, Carlos H. *Reversal of Development in Argentina: Postwar Counterrevolutionary Policies and Their Structural Consequences*. Princeton: Princeton University Press, 1987.

Walter, Richard. *The Socialist Party of Argentina, 1890–1930*. Austin: University of Texas Press, 1977.

Warren, Roland L. "German *Partilieder* and Christian Hymns as Instruments of Social Control." *Journal of Abnormal Social Psychology* 38 (1943): 96–100.

Weber, Max. *Economy and Society.* New York: Bedminster Press, 1968.

Wellhofer, E. Spencer. "The Mobilization of the Periphery: Perón's 1946 Triumph." *Comparative Political Studies* 7 (1974): 239–251.

Wilner, Ann Ruth. *The Spellbinders: Charismatic Political Leadership.* New Haven: Yale University Press, 1984.

Winter, Sydney G., Jr. "Concepts of Rationality in Behavioral Theory." University of Michigan, Institute of Public Policy Studies, Discussion Paper no. 7, 1969.

Wolfenstein, Martha. *Disaster.* Glencoe, Ill.: Free Press, 1957.

Wynia, Gary W. *Argentina: Illusions and Realities.* New York: Holmes and Meier, 1986.

———. *Argentina in the Postwar Era: Politics and Economic Policy Making in a Divided Society.* Albuquerque: University of New Mexico Press, 1978.

Zajonc, R. B. "Feeling and Thinking: Preferences Need No Inferences." *American Psychologist* 35 (1980): 151–175.

Ziv, Avner, Arie W. Kruglansky, and Shmuel Shulman. "Children's Psychological Reactions to Wartime Stress." *Journal of Personality and Social Psychology* 30 (1974): 24–30.

Index